BFI FILM CLASSICS

· ·

Rob White
SERIES EDITOR

Edward Buscombe, Colin MacCabe and David Meeker
SERIES CONSULTANTS

Cinema is a fragile medium. Many of the great films now exist, if at all, in damaged or incomplete prints. Concerned about the deterioration in the physical state of our film heritage, the National Film and Television Archive, part of the British Film Institute's Collections Department, has compiled a list of 360 key works in the history of the cinema. The long-term goal of the Archive is to build a collection of perfect showprints of these films, which will then be screened regularly at the National Film Theatre in London in a year-round repertory.

BFI Film Classics is a series of books intended to introduce, interpret and honour these 360 films. Critics, scholars, novelists and those distinguished in the arts have been invited to write on a film of their choice, drawn from the Archive's list. The numerous illustrations have been made specially from the Archive's own prints.

With new titles published each year, the BFI Film Classics series is a unique, authoritative and highly readable guide to the masterpieces of world cinema.

The best movie publishing idea of the [past] decade.
Philip French, *The Observer*

A remarkable series which does all kinds of varied and divergent things.
Michael Wood, *Sight and Sound*

Exquisitely dimensioned ... magnificently concentrated examples of freeform critical poetry.
Uncut

Editor's note: this book is the fiftieth to be published since the inception of the BFI Film Classics in 1992.

BFI FILM CLASSICS

TAXI DRIVER

·····················

Amy Taubin

bfi Publishing

First published in 2000 by the
BRITISH FILM INSTITUTE
21 Stephen Street, London W1P 2LN

The British Film Institute
promotes greater understanding
and appreciation of, and
access to, film and moving image
culture in the UK.

British Library Cataloguing-in-Publication Data
A catalogue record for this book is available from the British Library

ISBN 0–85170–393–3

Series design by
Andrew Barron & Collis Clements Associates

Typeset in Fournier and Franklin Gothic by
D R Bungay Associates, Burghfield, Berks

Printed in Great Britain by Norwich Colour Print, Drayton, Norfolk

CONTENTS

. . . .

To Paul Pavel (1925–1992),
who understood dreams too well to bother about movies.

ACKNOWLEDGMENTS

. . . .

I would like to thank Martin Scorsese and Paul Schrader for their generosity with interview time; Kent Jones and Gavin Smith for their help with accessing primary source materials; my assistants Helena Robinson, Gilad Melzer and Dara Schaefer for their research; J. Hoberman for his encouragement and especially for lending me his copy of Arthur Bremer's *An Assassin's Diary*; Mark Kelly for his explanations of the Catholic Mass; Rob White for his extraordinary patience and helpful editing; and, particularly, Paul Arthur for many conversations about subjects critical to this text, namely film noir, American history and the construction of masculinity.

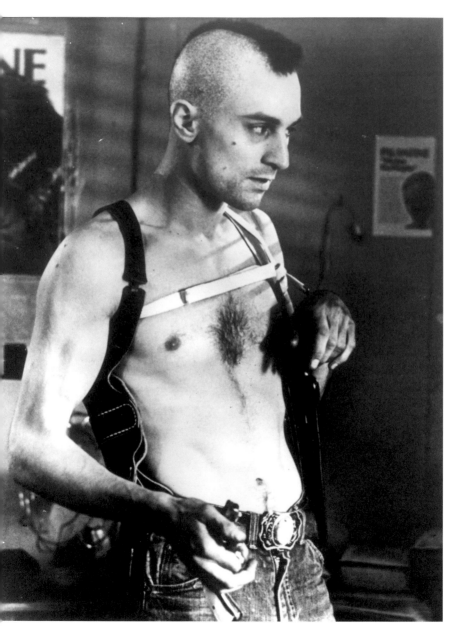

'TAXI DRIVER'

. . . .

Really, it is not violence at all which is the 'point' of the western movie, but a certain image of man, a style, which expresses itself most clearly in violence. Watch a child with his toy guns and you will see: what most interests him is not (as we so much fear) the fantasy of hurting others, but to work out how a man might look when he shoots or is shot. A hero is one who looks like a hero.

Robert Warshow, 'The Westerner'

The person who made that slanderous movie about cab-drivers should be taken out and shot.

Anonymous New York City cabbie, quoted by film critic Vincent Canby in the *New York Times*

I felt like I was walking into a movie.

John Hinckley III, explaining his state of mind during his attempted assassination of former US President Ronald Reagan

Perhaps the place to begin is with John Hinckley III, the man who, in 1981, tried to shoot President Ronald Reagan so that, as the defence explained at his trial, 'he could effect a mystical union with Jodie Foster', the actress who played a preteen prostitute in Martin Scorsese's *Taxi Driver* and who, at the time of Hinckley's assassination attempt, was a freshman at Yale University. Hinckley's action assured *Taxi Driver* a privileged position in cultural history, making it the only film to inspire directly a presidential assassination attempt. That the assassination failed is only fitting, since *Taxi Driver* is a film steeped in failure — the US failure in Vietnam, the failure of the 1960s counterculture and, most unnerving, at least to 49 per cent of the population, the failure of masculinity as a set of behavioural codes on which to mould a life.

Or perhaps the place to begin is a decade earlier, with Arthur Bremer, who, in 1972, attempted to assassinate Alabama Governor George Wallace, but merely succeeded in paralysing him from the waist down. The front page stories about Bremer, along with Sartre's *Nausea*, Dostoevsky's *Notes from the Underground* and Robert Bresson's film *Pickpocket* (1959), directly inspired Paul Schrader's *Taxi Driver* screenplay.[1]

Schrader read the Bremer coverage while he was in a Los Angeles hospital, recovering from a gastric ulcer, at what he describes as the low point in his life. He was twenty-six years old, his marriage had broken up, the affair that broke up the marriage had broken up, he had quit the American Film Institute where he had been a fellow and he had been living in his car and drinking heavily. He said that when he checked in to the emergency room, he realised that he had not spoken to anyone for weeks. No wonder his imagination was captured by Bremer, who was also totally isolated and living in his car while he stalked various political heavyweights. Coming of age in the aftermath of a decade of political assassinations (JFK, Malcolm X, Martin Luther King, Robert Kennedy), Bremer had convinced himself that the surest and fastest way for him to get the attention he was starved of was by assassinating a famous politician. When he failed to penetrate Nixon's security, he turned his attention to Wallace.

Bremer kept a diary. Parts of it were found in his car and parts in an apartment where he'd lived before taking off on the journey that would land him, at age twenty-one, in the penitentiary with a sixty-three year sentence. The diary wasn't published until 1974,[2] but passages from it made their way into the news stories. Schrader, who was already wedded to the first-person, voice-over narrative, found it fascinating that Bremer, an undereducated, lower middle-class, midwestern psychopath, would talk to himself in his diary just like a Sorbonne dropout in a Robert Bresson film.

Schrader got out of the hospital and wrote the script of *Taxi Driver* in about ten days.[3] 'The theme,' he says, 'was loneliness, or, as I realised later, self-imposed loneliness. The metaphor was the taxi, a metal coffin on wheels, the absolute symbol of urban isolation. I'd had this song by Harry Chapin in my head, about a cab driver who picks up a fare and it turns out to be his former girlfriend. And I put all that in the pressure cooker of New York City.' And who was Travis Bickle? Was he Arthur Bremer? 'Travis Bickle,' Schrader replied, 'was just me.'

In case there's anyone who doesn't know, *Taxi Driver* describes one stiflingly hot summer in the life of Travis Bickle (Robert De Niro), an alienated ex-Marine who drifted to New York shortly after the end of the Vietnam War. This background sketch may or may not be true, since we have only Travis's word for it. With small exceptions, the film is told from Travis's point of view and he is, to put it mildly, an unreliable narrator. Travis takes a job as a cabbie. Unable to sleep at night, he cruises in his taxi through a city that seems to him a hell. He becomes obsessed, in turn, with two women: Betsy (Cybill Shepherd), a campaign worker for a presidential primary candidate, and Iris (Jodie Foster), a twelve-year-old prostitute. Betsy is the Madonna Travis wants to turn into a whore, while Iris is the whore he wants to save.

The seemingly desultory narrative is rigorously divided into three acts. In the first, Travis's rage is diffuse; he rides around in his cab, more a witness than a man of action. In the second, he finds a mission and an object for his rage. ('One day, indistinguishable from the next, a long, continuous chain. And then, suddenly – there is change,' he writes in his diary.) In the third, he puts his homicidal fantasies into action, taking aim at one father figure (the presidential candidate) and, when that attempt fails, turning his gun on another (Iris's pimp Sport, played by Harvey Keitel). The carnage that ends *Taxi Driver* is devastating, but it's also voluptuous – as voluptuous as anything in American movies – and all the more so because of the sense of repression that pervades the film until this moment. The entire film has been built so that this eruption of violence would seem both inevitable and more horrific than anything we might have imagined.

. . . .

The slaughter is the moment Travis has been heading for all his life, and where this screenplay has been heading for more than eighty five pages. It is the release of all the cumulative pressure; it is a reality unto itself. It is the psychopath's Second Coming.

Paul Schrader, *Taxi Driver* screenplay[4]

I like the idea of spurting blood. It reminds me … God, it reminds me … it's like a purification … you know, the fountains of blood … like in the Van Morrison song … 'wash me in the fountain'. But it's realistic, too. The guy that puts the blood … I said, give me a little more, he said that's going to be a lot, I said that's okay.

Martin Scorsese, March 1976, a month after *Taxi Driver* opened in the United States[5]

Soon after Schrader wrote the first draft of *Taxi Driver*,[6] he showed it to Brian De Palma, who passed it on to the producers Michael and Julia Phillips. They optioned the script for $1000 and began peddling it to the studios. There were no takers. The script was considered too dark, too violent, its protagonist too unsympathetic. Scorsese was hot to direct the film, but the Phillips shrugged him off. *Mean Streets* (1973) changed their minds. Still, their commitment to Scorsese hinged on his ability to convince one of his *Mean Streets* stars, Robert De Niro, to play Travis. Financing remained elusive for two years. It wasn't until De Niro won an Academy Award for his performance in *The Godfather Part II* and Scorsese's direction of *Alice Doesn't Live Here Anymore* resulted in an Oscar for Ellen Burstyn that David Begelman, then president of Columbia, gave the Phillips a green light. Begelman loathed the script, but he couldn't refuse so much certified talent. *Taxi Driver* was financed originally for $1.3 million and wound up costing $1.9 million. Scorsese, Schrader and De Niro worked for next to nothing. Their up-front fees totalled $130,000. Scorsese and De Niro also had points in the picture, and, since the film grossed about $17 million in 1976 and ranked twelfth on *Variety*'s box office chart, they may have seen some small profit.

The violence Begelman found so disturbing in *Taxi Driver* had been working its way into Hollywood studio films for roughly two decades. Hitchcock raised the ante with *Psycho* (1960), which like *Taxi*

Driver, crossed the psychological thriller with the horror film. In *Alfred Hitchcock and the Making of Psycho*,[7] Steven Rebello writes that Hitchcock wanted to make a film to herald the new decade of the 60s. He had been tracking the box-office success of the low-budget horror films produced by American-International and Hammer Films. He was also slightly envious of all the attention that had been paid to a French-language art film, Clouzot's *Diabolique* (1955), with its gruesome corpse-in-the-bathtub scene. The trick, as Hitchcock saw it, was to adapt a déclassé piece of material (a pulp novel about a real serial killer), fill it with Hollywood stars and have it released by a major studio.

Although *Psycho* inspired an underbelly of slasher films, the studios were slow to follow Hitchcock's lead. The next major studio film to scandalise the Hollywood establishment and the middlebrow critics was *Bonnie and Clyde* (1967), which not only glamourised the eponymous outlaws, but also eroticised gun violence. Sam Peckinpah's *The Wild Bunch* followed two years later.

Bonnie and Clyde and *The Wild Bunch* opened against a background of the war in Vietnam and 'the war at home' – the civil rights and anti-war struggles. By 1968, the television networks, which had at first cooperated with the Pentagon by suppressing images of American dead or wounded, were pumping images of the escalating horror of the war – bodies that bled and burnt when assaulted by automatic weapons, bombs and napalm – into American households, where they were consumed as a regular part of the dinner hour. The imagery of the war and of the violence at home gave a moral justification to the film-makers, who now claimed it was their obligation, rather than their indulgence, to show the brutality of US culture. Also, in 1966 and again in 1968, the Motion Picture Association of America (MPAA) revised its rating code. More violence was allowed on screen, but age restrictions were placed on audiences.

The bloody nightmare of Vietnam surfaced not only in Hollywood movies, but also in avant-garde films and European art films. If *The Wild Bunch* was imprinted on Scorsese's retina, so too was Stan Brakhage's autopsy film, *The Act of Seeing With One's Own Eyes* (1971), and Jean-Luc Godard's *Weekend* (1967) and *Pierrot Le Fou* (1965). Indeed, it's *Taxi Driver*'s extraordinary hybridity that partially accounts for its influence on two generations of film-makers and artists.

There's a 1983 photograph by David Wojnarowicz (arguably the greatest and certainly the most subversive American artist of the 80s) which appears on the cover of the catalogue for his 1999 retrospective at New York's New Museum.[8] Wojnarowicz is seated in a chair, facing the camera. His right hand, with the index finger extended as if it were a gun, is pointed at his head. It's a mirror image of De Niro's gesture at the end of the massacre in *Taxi Driver*. Wojnarowicz's hand, however, is not covered in crimson. Instead, it's painted blue and his face is painted yellow – an homage to the ending of *Pierrot Le Fou*, where Belmondo, having just shot the woman he loves and bent on killing himself, paints his face blue and wraps yellow and red dynamite around his head.

Wojnarowicz made the connection between the suicidal, alienated anti-heroes of the two films, both driven mad by the time in which they lived, and between the striking use of primary colours in both films to describe a nightmare narrative – a male anxiety dream of castration and death. While there are no two more film-literate raiders of the image bank than Godard and Scorsese, their aesthetics, politics and methodology have little common ground. When Scorsese borrows the jump-cut strategy of *Breathless* (1959), it's not to shake up conventions of linearity or to throw a monkey wrench into habits of identification, but to reveal the gaps and disconnection in Travis's jumbled psyche.

If *Taxi Driver* owes something to French film of the 50s and 60s, it's even more influenced by American film noir, the genre the French New Wave adored. The stylistic influence is obvious in the first person voice-over narration, the expressionist camera angles and movements, and Bernard Herrmann's moody, jazz-inflected score. Unlike many of the neo-noirs that followed in its wake, however, *Taxi Driver*'s relationship to classic noir is more than stylistic. Like film noir, *Taxi Driver* is rooted in post-war trauma. What World War II was to noir, Vietnam is to the story of Travis Bickle.

In his influential 1971 essay 'Notes on Film Noir', Schrader describes how soldiers returning from World War II found a society 'less worth fighting for'. This disillusionment is directly reflected in such early noirs as *The Blue Dahlia* (1945) and *Dead Reckoning* (1946). Schrader's prophecies – that 'as the political mood hardens, the noirs of the 40s will become increasingly attractive' and that 'the forties may be to the seventies what the thirties were to the sixties' – proved true. [9]

The essay suggests but doesn't quite nail down the expression in film noir of an anxiety surrounding masculinity itself. That anxiety, which surfaced in the aftermath of World War II, was brought to the fore again in the 70s as a result of the feminist movement and the attention it focused on the construction of gender. The figure of Travis Bickle is an emblem of that masculine anxiety, and, as such, exerts enormous influence on the films of the next two decades, particularly on those of the 90s, a decade in which the 'white male backlash' and 'white male paranoia' became prime media topics.[10] While Scorsese's *Mean Streets* with its insider connection to a subculture never before depicted so accurately on the screen – arguably has been the most influential film worldwide for the generation of film-makers that followed, it's the character of Travis Bickle who opened the door to the new anti-hero, with his pathological relation to violence as the answer to the castration anxiety he barely troubled to hide.

The Vietnam war also intensified America's obsession with lethal weaponry. Americans have always cherished their constitutional right to bear arms, but the media coverage of the fighting gave guns a wider social currency than ever before. American gun fetishism is reflected in a century of movie making, beginning with the notorious shot at the end of Edwin S. Porter's *The Great Train Robbery* (1903), in which a black-hatted bandit stares down the audience, pulls the trigger of a revolver aimed straight at the camera and disappears in the smoke of the blast. In the early 70s, the .44 Magnum replaced the cherished .38 as the weapon that made the man. *Taxi Driver*'s ode to the .44 Magnum ('You should see what a .44 Magnum can do to a woman's pussy, that you should see …') is spoken not by Travis, but by a psychopathic passenger played by Scorsese himself. As an example of gun-craziness, it's a jump up from the speech that John Milius wrote for *Dirty Harry*'s Harry Callahan (Clint Eastwood): 'But seeing how the .44 Magnum is the most powerful handgun in the world and that it would blow your head clear off, you got to ask yourself – Do I feel lucky, today? Well, do ya, punk?'[11]

Critics of *Taxi Driver* regard it as an arty but right-wing offshoot of the vigilante films of the 70s, among them the *Dirty Harry* series, Phil Karlson's *Walking Tall* (1973) and Michael Winner's *Death Wish* (1974). But that critique ignores Travis's blatant psychopathology and his connection to the noir anti-hero. While the film evokes sympathy for Travis, it never suggests, as a vigilante film would, that he does the right thing. It's more to the point to think of *Taxi Driver* as an attempt to reclaim – for the embattled white male – the urban landscape that had been revitalised by the blaxploitation films of the early 70s. In that sense,

Schrader and Scorsese's project mirrors, however unconsciously, Travis's desire to clean the scum off the streets.

This is not to say that the director and screenwriter of *Taxi Driver* are racist in the way that Travis is. Rather it is that they are not above the impulse to protect what they consider their turf. Framed by the windows of his cab, New York looks to Travis like a movie. The entire cast of *Superfly* (1972) seems to have been assembled in Times Square. Seen through Travis's eyes, however, they're deprived of the agency and subjectivity they briefly enjoyed in the blaxploitation genre. They are once again objects, used merely as 'local colour'.

'You know the black man you see raging in the street late in the film, I wanted that to be the opening shot,' says Scorsese. 'But there was no way I could do that. It would have seemed too racist.'[12]

Racism is the problem with which *Taxi Driver* never quite comes to terms. And this evasion prevents it from being a truly great film, while allowing it a popularity that it otherwise would not have achieved. 'There's no doubt,' says Schrader, 'that Travis is a racist. He's full of anger and he directs his anger at people who are just a little lower on the totem pole than he is. But there's a difference between making a movie about a racist and making a racist movie. I love to make movies about people who are disapproved of by society because I feel if you can get people to identify with a character they don't think is worthy of identification, then you open them up in some way and who knows what happens once they open up.'[13]

Travis's racism is evident to anyone who looks at the film carefully. It's there in his body language when he's hanging out with a group of cab drivers, one of whom is black; it's there in his eyes when he's looking through the window of his cab at the action on the street. It is there, most overtly, when he shoots a skinny black junkie who's trying to hold-up a neighbourhood deli. It is not merely that Travis shoots to kill; it's the way he looks down at the dying man – as if the guy were not even human.

That particular scene is as close as the film comes to directly dramatising Travis's racism. Elsewhere it's displaced onto other characters (the psycho passenger played by Scorsese who's in a fury because his wife's lover is 'a nigger') or suppressed. In Schrader's

Travis guards the dying thief

original script, Sport (Iris's pimp) is black, as are the other men that Travis massacres in the hotel. 'When Marty and I started working together,' says Schrader, 'we got to the scene where Travis shoots Sport and we just looked at each other and we knew we couldn't do it the way it was written. We would have had fights in the theatre. It would have been an incitement to riot. There wasn't even a discussion about it. At that point, Marty sent me out to find "the great white pimp", but I never found him.'[14] What Schrader discovered instead was that streetwalkers like Iris were traded exclusively by black pimps. So much for *Taxi Driver*'s much-lauded documentary-style depiction of New York.

On his way to the 1976 Cannes Film Festival where *Taxi Driver* would win the Palme d'Or, Schrader stopped in Paris to interview Robert Bresson, who was one of his film-making idols.[15] Bresson asked him if he was pleased with *Taxi Driver* and Schrader responded: 'Yes, although it was not directed the way I would have directed it. I wrote an austere film and it was directed in an expressionistic way. I think the two qualities work together. There's a tension in the film that's very interesting.'

The tension between Scorsese's and Schrader's frames of references gives the film an ambiguity of meaning and affect. This ambiguity allows for a variety of readings and makes the film attractive to a wide audience. *Taxi Driver*'s appeal has something to do with the fact that Travis is largely a cipher that each viewer decodes with her or his own desire, and, also, with the fact that the more reprehensible aspects of Travis's character are played down by the film. Because of the disconnection between Travis's implicit racist fantasies and his explicit homicidal action, the effect of the film is the inverse of what Schrader claims. Travis winds up being more 'worthy of identification', precisely because the film deflects the consequences of his racism.

I suspect, too, that many viewers respond not to Travis's alienation per se, but, rather, to Scorsese's own sense of being an outsider in a glamorous city – expressed, not through character or narrative, but through *mise-en-scène*. Scorsese describes *Taxi Driver* as a mix of gothic horror and tabloid news, but it also has a high-end noir glamour. It's the glamour of New York that Bernard Herrmann's bittersweet theme expresses – a glamour that has rubbed off on the city from a hundred movies in which the sound of a soaring saxophone promises danger and love. Herrmann's score makes the film more pleasurable, but it's an uneasy fit with the first person construction of the narrative. At times it seems expressive of Travis's madness, but just as often it evokes experiences that are outside of Travis's reality.

Scorsese and Schrader were both raised in religious households: Scorsese as a Roman Catholic in New York, Schrader as a Calvinist in the Midwest. They agreed on the Christian allegorical aspect of Travis's story, but Scorsese sees him as a 'commando for Christ who goes too far; he has to kill you to save your life', while Schrader focuses on the problem of determinism and chance. Travis, however, is neither a Catholic nor a Calvinist. For the most part, he seems to have no interest in any religion. Although churches are everywhere in New York, he never notices them (and therefore they're absent from the film). But there's something in his language and, of course, in his dramatic trajectory that suggests the influence of an apocalyptic strain of Christianity, the kind of fundamentalist belief in the second coming that made Hal Lindsey's *The Late Great Planet Earth* the best-selling non-fiction book of the 70s.[16]

The difference between Schrader's and Scorsese's vision of Travis Bickle is encapsulated in their perspectives on John Ford's *The Searchers* (1956), the picture that is the ur-text for *Taxi Driver*, as well as for many other 70s films. When Scorsese talks about *The Searchers* in the context of *Taxi Driver*, he focuses immediately on the last shot: the lone figure of Ethan (John Wayne) walking away from the house and out onto the prairie, his back to the camera. 'The isolation, it must be unbearable,' says Scorsese.[17] He's reminded of an encounter he had in China with a young film student who'd seen *Taxi Driver* and told him that he understood Travis's loneliness because he was a very lonely person himself. Scorsese advised him to try to put some of his loneliness into his films. The student came back few days later and said that he'd followed Scorsese's advice, but that it didn't make him feel any less lonely. 'No,' said Scorsese, 'making a picture doesn't make the loneliness go away.'[18]

The scene in *The Searchers* which Schrader remembers most is 'John Wayne telling Jeffrey Hunter not to look'.[19] Ethan has come back from the canyon where he has found and buried the body of Debbie's older sister, who has been killed and most likely raped by the Comanche warrior Scar and his raiding party. What Ethan actually says to the men riding with him is: 'Long as you live, never ask me more.' If ever there was an invitation to viewers to let their imaginations run wild, that line is it. The rape fantasy aroused by Ethan's refusal to speak drives the rest of the narrative. *The Searchers* adds a blatant psychosexual component to the mix of fear and guilt that, in 'enlightened westerns', characterises the settlers' relationship to Indians. It's Ethan's fantasy of Scar making Debbie (Natalie Wood) his squaw that impels his seven-year pursuit.

Schrader's Travis Bickle is Ethan Edwards split open. In *The Searchers*, Ford finally shows the fissures in the masculine ideal he monumentalised. Ethan, too, is a man come home from a war in which he fought on the losing side. A racist who can't accept the defeat of the Confederacy and a misogynist who regards women as property and miscegenation as the ultimate crime, Ethan is also uncommonly courageous and loyal. In the end, his better side prevails, but, consumed with guilt, he can't allow himself to stay with the family he's reunited. Says Schrader, 'This is a man who's deprived of the pleasures of hearth and home because he has blood on his hands.'[20]

Ethan, the lone wolf, becomes Travis, the psychopath, trying to work out on his own what it is to be a man. Isolation intensifies his pathology. Quoting Thomas Wolfe, Schrader dubs him 'God's lonely man'. Like Ethan, Travis is driven by fantasies of rape and revenge in which he plays many parts. Schrader says a lot of pressure was placed on him (although not by Scorsese) to change the scene in which Travis takes Betsy, the woman he worships as 'an angel', to a porn movie on their first date. He was told that no one could be that stupid. On an unconscious level, however, Travis wants to rub Betsy's face in the muck and show her how bad he is. Although he could never admit it to himself, taking Betsy to a porn movie is a violation, a psychological rape. When Betsy gives him the cold shoulder, he redirects his desire towards Iris. This is where the model of *The Searchers* kicks in. Travis makes it his mission to rescue Iris from Sport – the hippie pimp who wears Indian beads and a bandana – even if it costs him his life.

In addition to his desire to 'forge a magical union with Jodie Foster', John Hinckley claimed, as part of his insanity defence, that sometimes he almost believed himself to be Travis Bickle, that he identified with Travis's loneliness and isolation, and that the movie, which he had seen fifteen times, had driven him mad. As the linchpin in their defence, Hinckley's lawyers screened *Taxi Driver* for the jury. Hinckley was found not guilty for reasons of insanity and was committed to a mental institution. In 1999, he began a programme of limited and supervised release. (As an example of the inequity of the US justice system, Arthur

Bremer, who could not afford anything approaching Hinckley's high-powered defence, was judged to be sufficiently sane to be responsible for his actions and is rotting in jail where he'll probably die.)

Whether the jury believed that Hinckley was mad to begin with and that *Taxi Driver* was merely icing on his paranoia, or whether they believed the film itself was the cause of his madness, is unknown. But what I would claim is that *Taxi Driver*'s power derives from its most hallucinatory scenes – the massacre in the hotel at the end and the 'You talkin' to me?' sequence where Travis challenges his mirror image. Both of these scenes involve some derailment of Schrader's screenplay and, indeed, of Scorsese's carefully storyboarded production plan.

Threatened with an X-rating because the film was too bloody, Scorsese, rather than making cuts, had the scene printed so that the blood appears less red. When Travis gets out of his cab to begin his 'rescue' mission, it's as if he's walking into one of the porn movies he watches obsessively when he can't sleep, but which has never before brought him release. Finally his murderous desire is as one with his action and his paranoid vision is so encompassing it colours the *mise-en-scène* itself.

The hallucination that Travis enacts in that scene – and which results in real death – is the hallucination of masculinity. It's the search for that image of ideal masculine wholeness that subtends the entire history of the movies. It's also what makes Scorsese's raids on the cinematic image bank not merely an aesthetic exercise in reflexivity, but also an expression of a dilemma that's both personal to Travis and bigger than Travis himself.

'A hero is one who looks like a hero,' wrote Robert Warshow in 'The Westerner'. But by the mid-70s, the ideal image of white masculinity was not merely fissured as in *The Searchers*; it had broken to bits under the pressure of the feminist and civil rights movements. In this context, Travis's paranoia can be read as a hyperbolic version of the doubts and defensiveness the average guy was feeling – continues to feel – about being a man.

The emblematic scene in which Travis confronts his own image in the mirror doesn't exist at all in the published version of the screenplay; in the shooting script, it's indicated only by a one-line description, 'Travis talks to himself in the mirror.' De Niro improvised the scene, drawing on the routine of a stand-up comic he'd seen in a downtown club. Scorsese, who was worried that the monologue would be inaudible because the location was so noisy, kept the camera running while De Niro repeatedly challenged and drew his gun on his own reflection.

The issues of identity and identification played out in this scene are insanely entwined in Travis, who, as a paranoic, has problems with boundaries and with splitting. When Travis looks in the mirror, he sees himself and he sees the other on whom he's projected everything he despises in himself. Thus, what Travis is doing when he 'is working out what it is to shoot or be shot' is rehearsing a murder that is also a suicide.

It's an action in which the audience is wildly implicated. The angle at which Travis takes aim at himself is only about ten degrees removed from the angle at which he would be shooting directly at the camera, that is, at us. Travis's disassociation, moreover, reflects the latent madness in the situation of viewers who lose themselves in a film, experiencing the fear and desire, love and hate of the character on screen as if it were their own. When the character is madly confused about his identity, identification packs a double whammy.

. . . .

Taxi Driver was shot in the summer of 1975 in what Scorsese recalls as 'forty days, forty nights'. Because the budget was tight, the production had to be rigorously preplanned. As with his previous films, Scorsese storyboarded every sequence. Six weeks before production began, Schrader wrote a final draft of the script. This is the version that is published by Faber and Faber. It differs from the film itself both in the order of scenes and in the dialogue. Some of these changes occurred when Scorsese worked with the actors on the set. Others were made during the editing process.

All film shoots are difficult, but *Taxi Driver* presented particular problems, the largest of which was New York itself. The summer of 1975 was extremely hot, the economic downswing was taking a heavy toll in both the private and public sectors, unemployment was high, the city's infrastructure was crumbling, and the underground economy of drugs and prostitution was booming.

Among the many reasons that *Taxi Driver* has become a classic is that it testifies to both a vanished New York (chequer cabs, rotary phones, typewriters and 3 a.m. coffee at the Belmore Cafeteria) and an absolutely contemporary anomie. The film's love/hate relationship with the city plays into the fantasies of both New Yorkers and those who project from afar their fears, loathings, hopes and desires. In 1996, when a restored print of *Taxi Driver* made the rounds of museums and

repertory houses in celebration of its twentieth anniversary, the disjunction between the New York depicted in the film and the actual New York was not nearly as great as it is today. The economic boom of the late 90s speeded up the rate of gentrification. The old Times Square district, which is geographically at the centre of the film and also at the core of Travis's paranoid vision, has been almost completely torn down and rebuilt as a monument to the corporate media culture – to Time-Warner, Disney, Bertelsmann and Condé Nast. Today, it's not the danger of pushers and pimps that makes long-time New Yorkers paranoid, but the dehumanisation of the very heart of the city – the sense that it has been taken over by the ultra rich, the automatons that toil for them and the type of tourist that prefers this urban Disneyworld to the neon nether world of porn theatres and strip joints.

Scorsese was no stranger to the old Times Square. As a teenage film buff, he ventured away from his neighbourhood of Little Italy (a neighbourhood which also all but disappeared in the 90s, metamorphosing into the trendy boutique and condo enclave dubbed Nolita) to watch western and horror double-bills in the run-down movie theatres that lined 42nd Street. As a film student and fledgling director, he also frequented the labs and production houses clustered in the Times Square district, some of which are still thriving today.

Applying the lessons he learned in the Catholic Church, Scorsese describes Travis's perambulations of the Times Square red light district as 'putting himself in the occasion of sin'. That's not Travis's terminology, Scorsese says, since Travis isn't a Catholic. Rather, it's a way that he, Scorsese, could get a handle on Travis's actions. Scorsese might have used that same phrase to describe his own adolescent Times Square adventures (some of his most cherished memories are of films that were banned by the Church) and, even more significantly, the enormous change in his life when, having left Fordham University where he was studying for the priesthood, he enrolled in film school at NYU.

If the New York of *Taxi Driver* is sin city in the eyes of the Church, it's also outside the control of another patriarchal authority – the Hollywood studio system. It wasn't only Schrader's script that disturbed the Columbia brass. The studios, in general, view any location that's more than an hour away by plane from Los Angeles as potentially dangerous. The more geographical distance a director puts between himself and the studios, the more that director might be tempted to break their rules. Because of his identification with New York, Scorsese was already viewed as something of a wild card, although, paradoxically, *Mean Streets*, his definitive New York movie prior to *Taxi Driver*, involved less than a week of New York location shooting.

Scorsese's ambivalent relationship with genre and to the studio system which functions as a surrogate father meshes with Travis's oedipal trajectory – with, on the one hand, his killing of the father and, on the other, his longing for organisation and for a normal life. All of Scorsese's loners yearn for some kind of orderly life from which they've been exiled or which no longer exists. *Taxi Driver* honours many fathers, from John Ford to Alfred Hitchcock, but it doesn't obey their rules. There's no way it can. Even if Scorsese were not subversive by temperament, the studio system that generated those rules had collapsed by the mid-70s. Still, what makes *Taxi Driver* an ur-text for the independent film-makers of the 80s and 90s is precisely its fraught relationship to an idealised Hollywood past.

. . . .

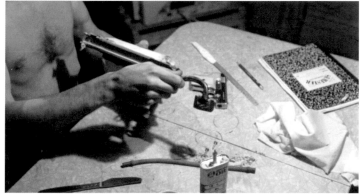

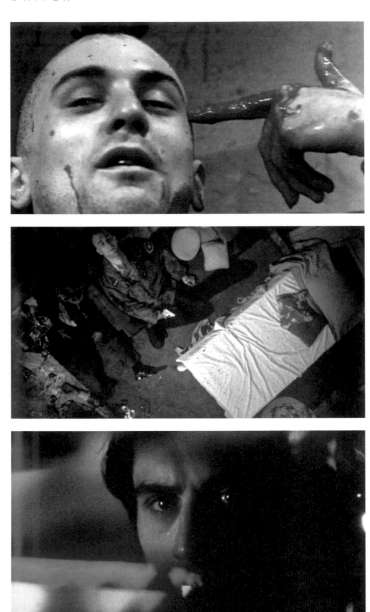

Certainly, *Taxi Driver* announces itself as a Hollywood studio film of a particular kind – the star vehicle. (In the context of this film, the term 'vehicle' carries a heavy load.) The first image we see is the inscription 'Columbia Pictures presents' in small red letters against a black background. The screen briefly goes black and then the larger red letters of the second title appears: 'Robert De Niro in'. As that title fades, an ominous sound of brass, side drums and cymbals is heard, the first of Bernard Herrmann's two basic musical themes.[21] This one has no melody to speak of; it's merely a descending two-note phrase which is treated throughout the film with various instrumental arrangements, harmonies and tonal densities. The sound swells and the screen is enveloped in white sewer vapours, which disperse just enough to reveal a yellow chequer cab gliding in slow motion and in close-up diagonally across the screen. The sound, the vaporous cloud, the slow motion and the low angle of the shot conspire to suggest that this taxi has just risen out of some underground inferno. For all its glistening chrome, it reminds us of nothing so much as the vampire's carriage in Murnau's *Nosferatu* (1921), the carriage which is introduced by one of the most chilling titles in all of cinema: 'And then the phantoms came to greet him.'

As the taxi moves out of frame, it seems to leave in its wake the title of the film, '*Taxi Driver*', which hangs on the screen against yet another billowing cloud of white. The titles continue and, through the diffusion of the vapours, we begin to distinguish the glow of street lamps, traffic lights and neon signs.

Then, suddenly, we see a pair of eyes filling the screen. The shot is tinted red as if coloured by the street lights; the effect quite lurid. The eyes are framed to take advantage of the wide screen ratio, framed as they might be by a taxi's interior rear view mirror (which is how we'll often see them later in the film). They are, at this point, 'eyes without a face' – the American translation of the title of Georges Franju's 1959 horror film, *Yeux sans visage*, which Scorsese undoubtedly had seen. But there's nothing horrifying about these eyes, or, at least, not in the first glimpse we have of them. They might be the eyes of a handsome romantic, an impression reinforced by the lilting saxophone melody that accompanies their first appearance. (The melody is the second of Herrmann's two themes, and, although it's as light in tone as the first theme is dark, it's nevertheless built around the same descending two note phrase.)

Now we see what those eyes are seeing: Broadway at night, through a rain-drenched windshield. As the titles and the saxophone continue, the point of view dissolves into an optically processed shot of the same location – the lights still jagged and smeared, although the wet windshield is no longer in the picture. The slow-motion image becomes more complicated as pedestrians crowd the street at the crosswalk. The final title, 'directed by Martin Scorsese', comes up, and again there's a close-up of the eyes as they shift slowly to the right and then to the left, scanning the traffic. This time, however, the glance is tinged with anxiety.

Just over two minutes in length, this elegant title sequence encapsulates the essential elements of *Taxi Driver* in regard to its *mise-en-scène*, its film lineage and its method of inscribing subjectivity. It suggests that what we're about to see is some kind of hybrid of an urban horror film, an urban road movie and a psychodrama with neo-noir overtones. It also suggests that the film will be dominated by a single subjective point of view filtered by and reflected in the windows and mirrors of a taxi from hell. Despite the fragmentation of the sequence, we sense that the man (of whom we've seen nothing but a pair of eyes) and the vehicle that encloses him are inseparable.

In the first scene after the title sequence – the opening scene of the film – Travis (Robert De Niro) applies for a job as a taxi driver. He enters the office of the taxi garage in a puff of sewer gas that merges with the cigarette smoke clouding the run-down interior. It's a weird little joke on the horror genre and a sign of the way the language of horror and the language of neo-realism will fuse in the film.

Most of what we will know about Travis's background is laid out in this perfunctory job interview. In answer to the dispatcher's questions, Travis discloses that he's twenty-six years old and that he was honourably discharged from the Marines in 1973. He's evasive about his education: 'Some – here, there', he says, a hint of shame creeping into what we can already discern is a habitual defensiveness. He says that because he can't sleep, he has been riding around the city at night in buses and subways, so he figures he might as well get paid for his travels.

It's difficult – both for us and for the taxi dispatcher – to get a read on Travis in this scene. Dressed in a brown waist-length military-surplus jacket, dark-patterned shirt, jeans and cowboy boots, he could be just about anybody. He has a good-looking face with high cheekbones,

regular features and wide-spaced deep-set eyes. Nothing about him is distinguishing except the anxiety that seems to come over him in waves, contracting the muscles around his eyes, causing him to freeze suddenly, like an animal who senses a predator nearby. The anxiety is out of proportion to the situation. It's a foregone conclusion that Travis is going to be hired for this job. There's always a need for cab drivers and especially for those who, like Travis, are willing to work nights and weekends, and to take passengers to what were then and are still now considered danger zones – Harlem and the South Bronx. (Although cab drivers are required by law to pick up all persons who hail them and to carry them to any destination they request within the five boroughs of New York City, many do not abide by the rules – witness the numbers of cabs that speed past anyone who's not white, particularly at night.)

Deceptively casual, this brief expository scene sets up the camera moves and edits that Scorsese will employ for most of the interactions between Travis and the other characters in the film. It's our first look at Travis and it's clear from the way he's positioned from the beginning to the end of the scene that he is the dominant presence. But Scorsese's directorial choices throw any simple notion of a first-person film narrative into question. While the taxi dispatcher's function in the narrative is limited to his interaction with Travis, he exists independently of Travis's perception. (This is the condition, as well, of all the other characters in the film.) Our understanding of Travis will accrue not only through what we see of his behaviour and what he tells us about himself, but also through the ways in which others react to him. It's important, therefore, that we not mistake the hard look the dispatcher gives Travis – as if he's seen something worrisome – for a paranoid projection on Travis's part. If Travis has the feeling that other people think he's weird, it's because they really do.

Although Scorsese will employ classic reverse-angle editing later in the film, here he favours off-centre compositions, surprise camera moves, jagged edits. The montage establishes Travis as the film's governing consciousness, but it allows us to see him through the eyes of others as well. The erratic rhythm of the editing suggests Travis's anxiety, which will build throughout the film to a full-scale psychotic break. Expressionist that he is, Scorsese want us to experience what Travis experiences. He wants to give us access to the state of Travis's soul.

In this respect, two shots are striking. The first, derived from horror films, is a kind of floating move into Travis's face as he reacts to the dispatcher reprimanding him for being a wise-ass. Travis's anger, like that of a poltergeist, draws the camera to him. The other shot is a brief overhead view of the dispatcher's desk as he hands Travis an application form. It's the first of a series of high-angle shots that will climax with the extended overhead tracking shot looking down on the carnage that Travis has wrought. The overhead shots give us a sense of Travis's disassociation. Here, it's as if Travis's gaze, mesmerised momentarily by the clutter of objects on the dispatcher's desk, had floated free of his body. Scorsese remarks that, for him, the overheads suggest looking down at the objects on the altar during the Catholic mass. He adds, as he did when he used the metaphor of Travis 'putting himself in the occasion of sin', that this is not necessarily Travis's frame of reference.

Exiting the taxi garage, Travis walks east on 57th Street. We see him in an extreme long shot that dissolves into a medium shot taken from the same angle. The dissolve in which Travis seems to disappear and reappear before our eyes is another version of his ghostly first appearance out of the cloud of sewer vapours. Scorsese says that the purpose of the dissolve is to nudge the film forward in time and to emphasise the discontinuities in

Travis's disturbed psyche. It's a steal, he explains, of a similar shot in a barroom scene in George Stevens's *Shane* (1952).[22]

The *Shane* reference adds another genre to *Taxi Driver*'s hybrid iconography, one that was missing from the title sequence. That genre, the western, is already embedded in Travis's name. Colonel William Barett Travis fought and died along with his entire company and the even more legendary Davy Crockett and James Bowie in the battle of the Alamo (1836) during the war between Texas and Mexico. Texas went on to win its independence, but the Alamo became a symbol of last-stand martyrdom and of a loss that needed to be avenged. Hence the rallying cry, 'Remember the Alamo.'

By virtue of his name, Travis is associated with 'the sacrificial myth of the last stand', which American historian Richard Slotkin argues is central to the interventionist western.[23] In *The Wild Bunch*, where the foray into Mexico is a metaphor for US imperialist intervention in Vietnam, Peckinpah demythologises the last stand, revealing its inherent pathology. In that sense, the film is generative for *Taxi Driver*.

Walking toward us on 57th Street, which in the early morning is as empty as a Texas prairie, Travis is carrying two centuries of American history written in blood. His claim to have served in the Marines in Vietnam may or may not be true. But it's not Vietnam alone that produced him. He is the product, rather, of the repetitive cycles of violence that have made the United States number one. What's most brilliant about *Taxi Driver* is that it locates, in Travis's pathology, the intersection of the individual psyche with history. Critical to this history is a particularly American strain of apocalyptic Christianity that sees, for example, the Alamo dead as Christian martyrs who will rise again. *Taxi Driver* is even more evasive about Travis's religious background than his military service, but there's no doubt that he fantasises himself as some kind of avenging angel.

To return to Travis, furtively drinking cheap brandy from a pocket flask to quell his demons: the shot of 57th Street has another, more practical, purpose. For anyone familiar with the geography of New York, it establishes the proximity of the taxi garage to the Times Square area, which is Travis's main cruising ground. On the level of the psyche, it's Travis's twisted desire (in Freud's system of the unconscious, his repetition-compulsion) that draws him night after night to the same neon strip of Broadway between Times Square and Columbus Circle. In terms of the geography of the city, however, it's logical that he would drive through this area looking for his first fare of the night. No matter how far he drives – Harlem, the Upper West Side, East 13th Street where he encounters Iris and where the massacre takes place – he always returns to the bright lights of the Fascination and Playland game parlours, to the blacked-out façade of Show World. They're the ground zero of his obsession, but it would be hard for him to avoid them even if he wanted to.

And now *chez* Travis: a circular pan reveals a dingy, messy one-room apartment. Prominent amid the clutter is a Vietnamese flag. We spy Travis's reflection in a mirror just before the camera finds him at a table writing. The scene introduces Travis's inner voice – the voice he uses in his diary. For this voice, with its paranoid delusions of grandeur, its contradictory assessments of self and others, and its pathological narcissism, the film is forever indebted to Arthur Bremer.

If 'outsider literature' were as accepted a category of aesthetic inquiry as 'outsider visual art', then *An Assassin's Diary* by Arthur Bremer would be ranked among the most stunning works of the genre. About 15,000 words in length, it comprises thirteen entries of varying length, covering a period of six weeks in the spring of 1972 when Bremer stalked first Richard Nixon and then George Wallace. The published diary, which ends two days before he shot Wallace, is not the entirety of Bremer's writings. After he was arrested, the police found more notebooks and papers in his apartment, among them a Travis-like page headed 'A Cretique [sic] of my Life,' in which he expresses a desire to be more organised. Bremer claimed to have buried another diary, which covered the winter of 1971–2, the period in which he bought the guns and the car he used in his assassination attempt. It was never found.

Bremer couldn't spell, and had only a rudimentary grasp of grammar, but his writing, fuelled by loneliness, frustration and longing for recognition, is haunting. The paranoid schizophrenia that Bremer suffered from mirrors the most perverse aspects of the society that rejected him. What he seems to have most wanted was simply to be noticed. 'This will be one of the most closely read pages since the Scrolls in those caves,' he writes. And a few lines later, 'ALL MY EFFORTS AND NOTHING CHANGED. Just another god Damn failure.'

Like Hinckley, Bremer claimed inspiration from a movie. He noted in his diary that he started thinking about making Wallace rather than Nixon his target while watching *A Clockwork Orange* (1971). While it would be foolish to deny the element of mimicry in both Bremer's and Hinckley's actions, the relationship of real life to the movies or the movies to real life is hardly straightforward. Schrader incorporated aspects of Bremer's journey towards annihilation and celebrity in *Taxi Driver*. Had he modelled the character of Travis more closely on Bremer, *Taxi Driver* would probably not have been made, much less have achieved its mythic status. Certainly John Hinckley III, who came from a wealthy oil industry family, never would have emulated Arthur Bremer. Only twenty-one years old when he shot Wallace, Bremer had a childlike vulnerability that Travis, who gives his age as twenty-six, had left behind. Bremer also had even fewer social skills than Travis and was much too strange in appearance to pass, as Travis does at first, for a regular guy. According to newspaper reports, he walked with a shuffling gait, head down, toes pointed outward. The people who remembered him described him as 'quiet' and 'a loner'. Bremer's only friend killed himself playing Russian roulette; the loss may have precipitated Bremer's psychotic breakdown.

Whereas Travis reveals himself on numerous occasions as someone who has been trained to kill, Bremer was incompetent at handling the guns he acquired with ease. He absent-mindedly left them in a bag in an airport bathroom. (They were returned by a helpful pilot.) Having forgotten that he had loaded his revolver, he fired a shot into his motel bed and was amazed that no one came looking for him. Crossing the Canadian border, he pushed one of the guns so far inside the chassis of his dilapidated car that he was unable to retrieve it. Bremer was a habitual bungler, but he also seems to have been, at least on an unconscious level, looking for someone to keep him from carrying out his plan.

More open in his yearning for sexual experience than Travis, Bremer devoted the longest entry in his journal to a description of his attempt to lose his virginity in a massage parlour during a trip to New York. (He was tracking Nixon at the time.) Each time he tentatively gropes the masseuse, she removes his hand from her body, saying that it's against the rules. Bremer obsesses about everything that the masseuse says and does, about what he could have done differently, and about his feelings which shift from hatred to envy to self-pity to pity for her, and back again. 'Thought [sic] I'm still a virgin, I'm thankful to Alva for giving me a peek at what it's like,' he writes. 'But earlier I was angry ... I stood close to her after it thinking that a horny man hates nothing so much as he hates a cock-teaser & that she would be a thief not to return a part of (or all of) the $30 ... But she kept it and complaimented [sic] me on my suit. I told her it was lousy. (Just a disguise to get close to Nixon. I wouldn't wear a ugly thing & spend $70 plus for it for any other reason.)'

When the judge pronounced a sixty-three year sentence, Bremer said that he 'would have liked it if society had protected him from himself'. While I have never had much of an emotional response to the character of Travis Bickle, I find it horribly sad that Bremer has rotted in jail for his entire adult life without the possibility of experiencing the sexual contact with a woman that he wanted so desperately. Perhaps that's sentimental of me, and perhaps it's precisely that kind of sentimentality that *Taxi Driver* refuses. I'm not sure.

Still, there's a power in Bremer's raw prose and in the direct contact it offers with his demented psyche that the film does not tap. Critic J. Hoberman, who used the Bremer diaries in *Vague Out on Main Street* (1974), a text and slide performance piece that he and his partner Bob Schneider created for their underground Theater of Gibberish, observed that the massage parlour scene is 'more incendiary' than anything in *Taxi Driver*. Scorsese has occasionally described *Taxi Driver* as a cautionary tale: 'It's not cautionary for psychopaths because you can't caution a psychopath, but cautionary for the society that produces them and casts them out and ignores them until it's too late.' If that were the only rationale for the film, then it would have to be said that *An Assassin's Diary* is more successful.

Schrader absorbed Bremer's inner voice (the diaries were heavily excerpted in the massive newspaper coverage of the shooting) and grafted it onto a character that, as he explained, was more or less himself at a very low point in his life. When De Niro came into the picture with his armoured body, his control freak posture and his imploded, collapsed-star affect, the flailing, childish Bremer was left far behind. In clinical terms, Bremer was a paranoid schizophrenic. Travis, on the other hand, suffers from a narcissistic character disorder. He's a classic 'borderline' personality, meaning that adverse conditions – isolation, war trauma, excessive alcohol and drug use, or maybe just driving a cab in New York – could push him over the edge into a paranoid psychosis.

As Travis's voice-over continues, the scene changes from his apartment to Times Square at night. We see the teeming street from his point of view inside the cab: first, a movie marquee advertising *The Texas Chain Saw Massacre* (1974), then a red neon 'Fascination' sign. The camera angle levels off and we begin to notice the people on the street: women in hot pants, halters and cheap wigs; a bunch of guys in undershirts lounging against a car. 'All the animals come out at night,' says Travis in his weary but basically affectless voice. The conceit of the film is that this is his inner voice, his diary voice, but the effect is that he's talking directly to us, taking us into his confidence, making us complicit in his litany of contempt: 'whores, skunk pussies, buggers, queens, fairies, dopers, junkies. Sick! Venal! Some day a real rain'll come and wash all this scum off the streets.' There's something biblical in the last line – a hint that Travis believes he's in the city of the Antichrist. The shots in this sequence are quite short and equal in length, their regularity underscored by the dirge-like beat of the music. Travis says he's working twelve hours a night, six nights a week and, although this driving montage is less than four minutes long, we sense from the inexorable rhythm of the editing how dulling the routine is. But dulled is exactly what Travis wants to be. As if to illustrate that what happens on the street and what happens in the back seat of Travis's cab are one and the same, the only passengers we see in this sequence are a businessman and a

After work, Travis cruises Times Square porn movies

prostitute going at it hot and heavy. Travis watches them in his rear-view mirror. They – along with the denizens of Times Square, the performers in the porn movie which Travis goes to in a desperate attempt to relax after work and the models in the X-rated magazines which litter the floor of his apartment – are part of a single world that Travis loathes, but from which he can't tear away his eyes.

Scorsese frames this world as if all of it is a movie. Inside his cab, Travis is as much a spectator as he is in his seat in the nearly empty porn theatre. The windows and mirrors of the cab turn the real world into a reflection that he observes without being observed. The cab is the best seat in the house, but it's also Travis's protection, his armour. Its windows are his eyes, its metal body his hardened torso. Driving his cab, Travis is on patrol in the way a cop or a soldier is on patrol – their vehicles their defence from the hostile 'other' outside.

'There's a man on the screen who's a fucking vehicle,' said Scorsese of Travis. The taxi is a perfect metaphor for Travis's paranoid psyche because while it armours him, it also leaves him vulnerable to attack – specifically to penetration from the rear. Scorsese described how vulnerable he felt when he spent a few nights riding in the front seat of a cab next to De Niro who was preparing for his role by actually working as a cabbie. 'It was frightening,' said Scorsese. 'You have no idea who's getting inside.'

The movie that Travis sees through his taxi windows resembles the kind of documentary photography that came into style in the 70s (the work of Bruce Davidson, for example, particularly his book *Subway*). Shot with a flash, these photographs have dense blacks, saturated colours, and an overall shine. It's a more sophisticated look than the tabloid effect that Scorsese claims was his intent. For the shots of the street from Travis's point of view, a taxi was rigged with multiple camera mounts inside and out. And although Scorsese makes a neo-realist use of New York, incorporating bystanders into shots, *Taxi Driver* is still a far cry from a documentary like Alan and Susan Raymond's *The Police Tapes*, which was made in the same year as *Taxi Driver* and which views the city largely from the back seat of a police car through the lens of a hand-held, low-end video camera. Almost every shot in *Taxi Driver* is calculated in terms of filmic expression and razzle-dazzle.

We are already ten minutes into the film when the first obvious plot element kicks in. The opening chapter of the film, which depicts Travis at work, ends with him lying on his bed. The camera rises and, tipping slightly, hovers above him. It's a small move, but it's odd enough to make you wonder what Travis has in mind when he says in voice-over: 'I don't believe that one should devote one's life to morbid self-attention. I believe that someone should be a person like other people.'

Travis immediately puts his thought into action by becoming obsessed with Betsy, a tall, blonde young woman whom he spies outside the Charles Palantine campaign headquarters near Columbus Circle. (At Columbus Circle, the sleazy Times Square district gives way to the up-scale neighbourhoods bordering Central Park.) Betsy enters the film in slow motion and bathed in sunlight. Travis fantasises that she's 'an angel' and that 'They can not touch her'. Scorsese superimposes this phrase, as it's scrawled in Travis's diary, over a shot of Betsy disappearing into the Palantine's large glassed-in ground-floor offices. (He says it was a steal from a moment in Godard's *Contempt* (1963).)

The scene that follows Betsy's first appearance takes place inside Palantine headquarters. As Betsy banters with Tom (Albert Brooks), her

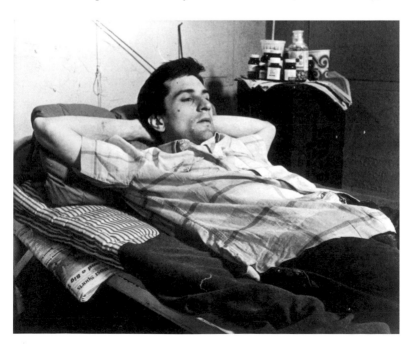

Travis contemplates becoming 'a person like other people'

co-worker, she reveals herself as both more banal and more ambitious than she is in Travis's love-at-first-sight fantasy. Unlike the elliptically edited opening ten minutes, this scene takes place in more or less real time and is a bit over three minutes long. It's deliberately three minutes of nothingness. Although it functions as comic relief, the scene also underscores the enormous difference between Travis's claustrophobic, anxiety-ridden existence and the chirpy white-bread world to which Betsy belongs. Breaking off their conversation, Betsy calls Tom's attention to the cabbie, who, she says, is parked outside and staring at them. When Tom approaches Travis, he realises that he's been caught looking and speeds away.

Driving at night, lovesick Travis notices couples making out in doorways. When he joins a group of cabbies in a twenty-four-hour coffee shop, they jokingly call him a ladies' man. Travis is as ill at ease with his peers as he will prove to be in almost all other company. Scorsese emphasises his isolation by framing him so that he's slightly apart from the others. Either he's alone in the frame or, in wide shot, he's at the far end of the table with a noticeable space between him and the group. It's clear that Travis would like to participate, but he doesn't know how to make small talk.

Introduced to Charlie T., the only black driver at the table, Travis averts his eyes, barely able to conceal his hostility. Despite the presence of Charlie T., the cabbies discuss the perils of driving in Harlem. 'Fuckin' mau-mau land,' says Wizard (Peter Boyle), the philosopher of the group. Travis turns to stare down three black pimps in Superfly regalia at another table. Then he dumps an Alka-Seltzer tablet in a glass of water. The camera moves in on the bubbling surface until it nearly fills the frame. The shot is another Godard reference (this one to the coffee-cup shot in *Two or Three Things I Know about Her* [1966]), but, like the overhead shots of objects on tables which recur throughout the film, it also suggests that Travis has become disassociated for a moment. Something is bubbling in Travis, but he doesn't know what it is. One of the cabbies asks Travis if he carries a gun. He answers that he doesn't; the idea, however, has been planted.

We're back in Palantine headquarters. Travis has come to volunteer, or so he says. Leaning over Betsy's desk, he confesses that he doesn't really have time to work for Palantine. What he wants is to take her out for coffee. Travis is as earnest and charming as we've ever seen him. Betsy agrees to meet him on her break.

Travis the outsider with other cabbies

Travis volunteers to Betsy

At a table in Child's coffee shop, overlooking Columbus Circle, Travis talks almost non-stop to Betsy, who seems puzzled but intrigued by him. Betsy starts talking about organisational problems in her office and Travis switches the conversation to his personal problems with organisation (it's an Arthur Bremer moment). When he tells her that he senses a connection between them, she doesn't disagree. She says she's never met anybody like him. Perhaps Betsy's looking for novelty, perhaps she has too little experience with men outside her class to be able to discern that what's strange about Travis isn't simply a matter of being uneducated and knowing nothing about pop culture. As if to emphasise how hard Travis is trying to act like a regular guy, Scorsese limits the *mise-en-scène* to classical reverse angles and two-shots.

This is a very delicate scene. If Travis were to become overtly agitated, Betsy wouldn't agree to see him again. Given everything we know about Travis, however, it's hard to believe that he wouldn't become paranoid in such a stressful situation. And, in fact, there is one brief moment in which Travis turns hostile. Betsy tells him that he reminds her of a song by Kris Kristofferson: 'He's a prophet, he's a pusher, partly truth, partly fiction, a walking contradiction.' 'I'm no pusher,' Travis says angrily. Betsy replies that it is the 'walking contradiction' that applies to him. Travis's anger dissipates. He asks Betsy if she'll go to the movies with him and she doesn't refuse.

Preparing for his date with Betsy, Travis buys a copy of the Kris Kristofferson album she mentioned. That night, one of his fares turns out to be Charles Palantine. Travis tells him that he should clean up the city. 'This city is like an open sewer. The president should flush it down the fucking toilet.' Travis's rant is so violent that it's as if he's vomiting the filth he's obsessed with all over Palantine. He's also smiling in the way that he does around authority figures. We saw this smile in the early scene with the taxi dispatcher. It's a shit-eating grin mixed just a hint of predatory bared teeth. Realising that Travis is seriously disturbed, Palantine tries to humour him. Travis knows he's being humoured and it pisses him off, but the ride ends without confrontation.

Later that night, Travis is parked on Third Avenue and 13th Street (a block notorious for under-aged prostitutes). A young girl in a white floppy hat and white hot pants jumps in the back seat. But before Travis can drive off, she's pulled out of the cab by a guy who throws a crumpled $20 bill onto the front seat. After the guy yanks on the girl's arm, there's a cut to a close-up of Travis's wary eyes reflected in the front rear-view mirror. It's the most extreme close-up since the opening title sequence. It tells us that Travis has registered this interaction in a big way. Later, we'll discover that the girl is Iris and the guy is her pimp Sport. What's crucial at this moment is that Travis's encounter with Sport immediately follows his encounter with Palantine. Henceforth, they're associated in Travis's warped psyche – two men whom he resents because they hold women in thrall.

Back in the garage, Travis sees the crumpled bill lying on the front seat. He stares at it for few seconds and then shoves it in his pocket. It's yet another moment where Travis's disassociation is revealed through a fixation on an inanimate object. We see the bill lying on the seat. The camera rises to take in Travis's face and then drops down to the bill again. The move looks simple, but Scorsese remarked that they had to do about twenty-five takes to get it right.

It's late afternoon and we see Travis on the street, shot with a long lens that isolates him from the rush-hour crowd. Travis is dressed up in a sports jacket and tie. He's on his way to meet Betsy for their movie date. He's shown in slow motion, just as Betsy was when she made her entrance into the film. The slo-mo suggests that Travis is so euphoric that his feet don't touch the ground. But Travis's bliss is short-lived. Betsy is upset by his choice of movie. Travis takes her to *Swedish Marriage Manual*, a porn movie playing on 42nd Street. Betsy takes one look and flees the theatre. Outside, she ignores Travis's pleas and leaps into a cab alone.

Travis is alone in the back of the lobby of an office building. He's talking to Betsy on a pay phone. From what we hear him say, it's clear that she's giving him the brush-off. Midway through the conversation, the camera tracks away from Travis. When it comes to a stop, we still hear Travis's pleading voice, but all we see is the empty lobby corridor. Scorsese says that this was the first image he pictured when he started working on *Taxi Driver*. In the oeuvre of a director who defines film as movement, the shot is an anomaly. Its stillness is the stillness of death. The long, narrow corridor seems like a coffin. The four elevator doors along the left wall and the bronze mailbox on the right wall are like coffins within a coffin. Looking at this image, we have a sense of the way everything inside Travis freezes when Betsy rejects him. The abandonment he feels is enough to stop his breath. The camera stays motionless as Travis re-enters the frame and walks towards the door. The

dejected curve of his back says more than any close-up. As he walks, we hear his voice-over, his account of what happens over the next few days – how Betsy refuses his calls and sends back his flowers unopened.

But Travis refuses to take no for an answer. Barging through the doors of Palantine headquarters, he confronts Betsy and berates her for 'being like all the others'. When Tom attempts to eject him, Travis instantly drops into a menacing karate crouch. It's the first evidence that Travis is a trained killer, that his story about being in the Marines may be true. (Another possibility is that he learned his commando techniques in some underground right-wing militia group.) We've known all along that he's potentially dangerous. This scene brings that potential into the here and now. And the intensity of his rage raises the narrative stakes. Among the many remarkable aspects of De Niro's performance is the way he continues to suggest until the very end that we haven't yet seen the worst of Travis. In this scene, Travis is still trying to hold himself together. It's like watching someone trying to cork an exploding bottle.

As Travis stomps down the street in a fury, we hear him obsessing about Betsy in voice-over, as if the voice had leaped ahead of the action, as if he were already writing in his diary. 'I see now that she's like the others. Cold and distant. Many people are like that, women for sure.

They're like a union.' That's a bombshell appraisal. It tells us Travis is angry not just at Betsy, but at women in general. And it suggests that he unconsciously sabotaged his relationship with Betsy (which was unlikely to begin with) by taking her to a porn movie so that she would reject him like 'all the rest'.

A few more words here about the voice-over, which weaves in and out of the action throughout the film. Scorsese often uses voice-over, but not as he does here. In *Mean Streets* and *Goodfellas* (1990), the voice-over is cast in the past tense. The voice is that of the protagonist, who leads us through the story. He's not omniscient, but he has learned from his experience. Travis's inner voice lacks that kind of comprehension. Travis is trying to figure out his life as it happens and what he doesn't understand about himself is more revealing than what he does.

The primary function of the voice-over in *Taxi Driver* is to leak information to us about what's going on inside Travis. Judged purely in terms of his actions, Travis might seem like a pitiful schizophrenic or a reprehensible sociopath. The voice-over makes us aware of something more disturbing – that his frustration and rage is on a continuum with our own. The problem with *Taxi Driver*, however, is not that it gives Travis his humanity, but that it deprives others of theirs. Betsy has been subjected to something close to date rape; however, because the film privileges Travis's subjectivity, we're left with the impression that she was left almost unscathed, and perhaps even that she got what she deserved for slumming. And the film is rigged in Travis's favour in yet another way. Like all those who incur his wrath, Betsy is not an appealing person. In the script, Schrader labels her a star-fucker, plain and simple. Shepherd brings a bit more complication to the character. Her brittle manner doesn't quite cover her wounded narcissism and the resultant anger, which she long ago learned to swallow. Still, she's the type of person who, when she talks to you, is always on the lookout for someone better.

Using Bresson as a model, Schrader varies the placement of the voice-over: it can be in sync with the action, lag behind it or push ahead. Most often, the voice-over bridges events that might otherwise seem tenuously connected or forced in their coincidence. Paranoids characteristically find causality in coincidence and evidence of master plans in randomly synchronic occurrences. By using Travis's voice-over as connective tissue, Schrader's script turns syndrome into narrative. As a cab driver, Travis's working hours are governed by chance – more so than they would be in most other occupations. As a paranoid, Travis turns chance into pattern. By making a paranoid cab driver his protagonist, Schrader transforms the movement of chance into a tightly organised narrative, an urban ethnography in which there are no loose ends and everything is accounted for. There's a link between Schrader's Calvinist determinism and the perverse determinism of paranoid thought.

Thus, it's as if Travis's murderous thoughts about Betsy conjured the maniacally jealous husband who's the next passenger in his cab. When the actor who had been chosen to play this tasty role was seriously injured while working on another film, Scorsese substituted himself. He claims to have had no choice since he had already used up his entire A-list of character actors in other small parts. It would be paranoid to suspect that the substitution was other than serendipitous, but the result is that that particular scene takes on a layer of meaning it otherwise wouldn't have had.

When it's the director of the film talking about blowing a woman to bits with a .44 Magnum because she's having an affair with a 'nigger', the words carry more weight than they would if said by a day-player. Scorsese articulates what Travis refers to as the bad thoughts in his head, the thoughts he can't bring himself to put into words – leaving him in the end no choice but to put them into action. Travis is a classic case of the repressed returning as apocalypse.

Watching these two, you have to wonder which is the more crazy. Scorsese's character is on a speed rant, stuttering and repeating himself, revving his rage with the sound of his own voice. 'Did you ever see what a .44 Magnum pistol can do to a woman's face? Fucking destroy it. Blow it right apart. Now, did you ever see what it can do to a woman's pussy? That you should see. What a .44 Magnum pistol can do to a woman's pussy, you should see.'

Travis sits absolutely still, as if the slightest move might unhinge the passenger even more. Again, we have the sense that Travis is experienced in this kind of potentially deadly situation. But it's also as if the passenger is speaking Travis's thoughts, as if he has siphoned the words out of the back of Travis's head and into his own mouth. This is a crucial scene not only because it articulates an extremity of misogynist and racist rage, but also because it eroticises gun violence. The gun is a remedy for the castration anxiety that Travis and the passenger share. It's the weapon to use on those who make you feel less of a man.

The music takes an ominous turn during this bizarre tête-à-tête. The descending two-note phrase around which the two main themes are built is extended into a figure of four descending semitones, announced softly at first by clarinets and then repeated in a lower register by the brass. It suggests Travis's feeling of being sucked down into his own repressed rage. Herrmann would repeat and then develop this four-note phrase throughout the rest of the film.

On a break, Travis goes for coffee at the Belmore (the all-night cafeteria that was a favourite cabbie hang-out). Already seated around a table are the four drivers from the earlier coffee break scene. Once again, they're exchanging anecdotes about freaky events they've witnessed in the course of a night's work. Travis is so wired that you can almost see the hair standing up on the back of his neck. He can't conceal his hostility towards Charlie, the black driver. As he leaves, Charlie, points his finger at him as if it were a gun and says, 'See ya, killer.' Charlie's an experienced guy – we've already seen him brush off casually racist remarks – but what he sees in Travis is something more dire.

Outside the Belmore, Travis crosses paths with a group of rowdy black teens and a hooker mom with her kids (an unlikely group to find late at night in this neighbourhood). The near confrontation increases Travis's anxiety. He tries to tell Wizard that he's flipping out, but he keeps stopping himself mid-sentence. Wizard has seen just about everything in his twenty years of driving, and it has given him a live-and-let-live attitude, or perhaps he was that way to begin with. He sees that something is wrong with Travis, but doesn't want to admit to himself how serious it is. So, instead of probing, he gives him a rambling pep talk and prescribes getting laid and enjoying life a little. 'You have no choice,' says Wizard (who sounds in this scene like the mouthpiece for Schrader), 'because we're all fucked in a way.' He laughs at his own philosophising, shakes Travis's hand and sends him off with an encouraging, 'You're all right killer, just relax.'

At home, Travis watches Palantine on an old black-and-white television. Palantine's campaign rhetoric sounds more like gibberish and certainly more presumptuous than Wizard's advice. 'The people are rising to the demands I put on them.' Herrmann's ominous four-note phrase repeats again and again as Travis eats his version of comfort food – cheap apricot brandy and sugar poured over a bowl of white bread and milk.

Travis crosses paths with rowdy teens

'We're all fucked': Wizard advises Travis

Back on the job, Travis drives past Palantine headquarters. There's a sign in front that says 'Just Four More Days'. It might as well be prophesying the end of the world. By now we're familiar with Travis's routine. It's daylight when he starts and ends his shift, but mostly he drives by night. And it's night when he's forced to brake suddenly for two girls who have heedlessly crossed in front of him. Through the windshield, he locks eyes with one of them – it's Iris, the pubescent hooker in the white floppy hat who had earlier sought refuge in his cab.

As Travis drives slowly alongside the two girls, a black man (Frank Adu) rushes along the street in the opposite direction, screaming 'I'm going to kill her, I'm going to kill her', over and over again. The man's rage is so intense and so real that, for a moment, it cracks the veneer of the sleek and streamlined aesthetic object that is *Taxi Driver*. Unlike some of the street people, however, this particular man is an actor, and the brief appearance of his character is noted in Schrader's script. Echoing the jealous husband, the man gives voice to Travis's anger at Betsy for rejecting him. It's as if the entire city is infected with homicidal rage. For the girls, however, the black man is just part of the scenery. It's Travis, stalking them in his cab, who has them worried.

Travis follows the girls as they pick up two johns. Then he floors the accelerator and takes off. The close encounter with Iris intensifies Travis's anguish. 'All my life I've been alone … I'm God's lonely man,' he says in voice-over. It's unthinkable for Travis to follow Wizard's advice – to pick up Iris and get himself laid. Instead, he buys some guns.

This is the turning point in the film. Travis's diary entry: 'The days move along in an endless chain, one day indistinguishable from the next … And then there is change.' Travis goes to a cheap hotel room with 'Easy Andy' (Steven Prince),[24] the gun salesman. The camera glides across the merchandise laid out on the bed, while Andy enumerates each gun's virtue in his nervous, reedy voice. 'Isn't that a little honey?' he queries encouragingly, as Travis fits a small World War II souvenir in his belt. Travis tries out each gun, pointing one, then the other out the window, swinging around and pointing them in our direction. Although the first slow, gliding track along the .44 Magnum is shocking, the scene is quite low-key. Still, its erotic undertone is unmistakable. It is probably the most stunning example of gun fetishism in the history of cinema and the phallic connotations are blatant. It's as if Travis was being offered cocks of every shape and size. He buys them all.

Travis is enraptured by the display, and so is Scorsese, who is also practising a bit of cinematic one-upmanship. As Christopher Sharrett notes in his essay 'The American Apocalypse: Scorsese's *Taxi Driver*',[25] each of the guns Travis buys references a specific macho hero: the Magnum is favoured by Dirty Harry, the Walther PPK and the .25 automatic by James Bond, the snub nose Smith and Wesson .38 by Mike Hammer. The element of reflexivity gives the scene a certain distance, but it's disturbing nevertheless. When Travis tries out one of the guns, aiming it out the window at a passer-by, it doesn't seem as if he's in on the joke.

The film begins to accelerate. In a series of ritualistic scenes, Travis gets his body in shape with push-ups and pull-ups. Pain is the game. He holds his hand over an open stove burner. He practises at a shooting range. This is assassination as labour, a perverse tribute to Bresson's *A Man Escapes* (1956). The tone of the film grows more ominous. Again, we hear the low brass chords. The overhead cutaways – of Travis on the floor doing push-ups, of the guns laid out on a red cloth – appear more

Travis buys some guns

frequently, the sign that Travis's disassociation is intensifying as he armours his body.

In the porn theatre, Travis cocks his finger like a gun at the screen. We don't see the image he sees, but we hear the sounds of faked sexual passion. Again, the connection is made between gun violence and orgasm. But Travis doesn't come in his seat in the porn theatre. Nor does he come when he's sitting in the front seat of his cab, where the windows and mirrors frame a porn movie as epic as the city itself. I think it's safe to say that Travis never comes to orgasm, that, for him, the only possible release is death; the film will deprive him even of that and, by so doing, deprive us of the security of closure.

Less than half a minute in length, the porn theatre scene flashes by like a cutaway, but it's as much a touchstone for the film as the opening credit sequence. Not only does it connect Travis the voyeur to Travis the man of action – even if at this point the action is only play-acted – but it also does so in relation to the cinematic experience itself. When Travis cocks his finger at what we assume is a fornicating couple, he's acting out the fantasy of the jealous husband passenger. Travis is imagining his finger as a .44 Magnum blasting open the pussy on the screen. The scene also elides the porn movie (which we're forced to imagine because we never actually see it) and the noirish vignette that Scorsese, in his guise as the jealous husband, directs from the back seat of Travis's cab. As Scorsese commands Travis to 'see, up there', the camera pans slowly across the shadowy building façade until it reaches and holds on a lighted window which frames, as if it were a movie screen, the silhouette of a scantily dressed woman. The image fuels the passenger's rage just as the porn movie does Travis's.

After Travis points his finger like a gun at the screen, he lifts his hand to his head, resting his middle finger horizontally just below his eye and his index finger just above. He moves the middle finger up and down, opening and closing his field of vision. It's the same gesture that Charlie (Harvey Keitel) uses in *Mean Streets* when he's in the hotel room with his epileptic girlfriend and she asks him not to watch her getting undressed. The gesture itself is a turn-on, intensifying voyeuristic pleasure by repeatedly enforcing and breaking the prohibition against looking. But it's also similar to the gesture directors make when they are trying to frame a shot, using their hand as a viewfinder. The camera and the gun are imagined as comparable instruments for channelling the passive aggression of voyeurism into action.

As Travis repeats the gesture of cocking his finger at the screen, we hear him say in voice-over: 'The idea had been growing in my head for some time. True force. All the king's horses couldn't ...' The scene shifts back to Travis's room, now with a large Palantine poster nearly covering one wall. Travis is shirtless. From the waist up, his body is so muscled and compacted it looks like a weapon in itself. He has guns strapped on both sides of his torso and he practises drawing on himself in the mirror. The music has dropped out and we're aware of the ambient sound – televisions, music, sirens. Travis cuts a metal arm slide for one of the guns and tapes it to his forearm. Just as Travis doesn't simply drive a cab, he also doesn't merely carry a gun. He fuses flesh and metal into a killing machine.

At an outdoor Palantine rally, Travis ignores Betsy's presence and engages a tall Secret Service agent in conversation. Travis is wearing a military jacket with a King Kong company emblem on the sleeve. He has a goofy grin on his face and he looks like a nut job. The grin is an exaggerated form of the one we've seen whenever he has to deal with authority. But here, it's Travis who pushes the confrontation. Basically, he's daring the agent to do something. Since there's no law against acting weird, the agent has no recourse except to take a photo of Travis as he leaves.

Back at home, Travis continues practising in front of the mirror 'how a man might look when he shoots or is shot'. This is the 'you talkin' to me?' scene, arguably the most quoted scene in movie history. De Niro borrowed the signature line from a stand-up comic and it has become something of a cross for him to bear. Hardly a day goes by without some stranger tossing the phrase in his face as a sign of recognition.

In the near twenty-five years since the film's release, the mirror scene has taken on a life of its own. It has become a fetish object – an emblem of besieged masculinity making a defiant last stand. The fetishisation is, in part, a response to the fetishism inherent in the scene itself. 'Fetishism, broadly speaking, involves the attribution of self-sufficiency and autonomous powers to a manifestly man-derived object,' writes Laura Mulvey.[26] 'It is, therefore, dependent on the ability to disavow what is known and replace it with belief and suspension of disbelief.' In Freud's theory of the psyche, what sets this complicated mechanism in motion is specifically castration anxiety.

Challenging his reflection in the mirror, Travis disavows its status as an image, endowing it with autonomous powers. He turns his reflection into an opponent in order to prove to himself that he's the

Travis transforms himself

Travis fuses flesh and metal

Travis engages in conversation

better man. The image in the mirror is simultaneously Travis and not Travis. We are witnessing someone in the throes of a psychotic break practising a murder that is also a suicide.

Travis's action in the mirror scene fits the pattern Robert Warshow describes in his celebrated essay 'The Westerner'.[27] He is indeed working out 'how a man might look when he shoots or is shot'. Where Warshow claims that violence as a style can exist independently of 'the fantasy of hurting others', however, the mirror scene suggests the reverse. What's disturbing about the scene is precisely the fantasy of blood-letting behind the play-acting.

Scorsese stages and edits the scene so that Travis's disorientation and (mis)identification become our own. The mix of jump cuts, reverse angles and 180-degree swish pans make it difficult for us to distinguish Travis from his mirror image. To add to the anxiety, we are positioned almost directly in the line of fire. Thus, when Travis inquires 'You talkin' to me?', he's barely ten degrees away from looking us straight in the eye. It's as if Travis implicates us in his paranoid confusion of self and other, and of projection and reflection. If we are his mirror, then he is ours.

Travis is in his neighbourhood bodega when a skinny black junkie attempts a hold-up. The junkie has a gun in his hand and he's panicky enough to use it, but Travis fires first and the junkie goes down. As he slumps to the ground, Travis steps on the junkie's hand to keep him from firing, but it's clear the guy is already dead or dying. Travis tells the storekeeper that he doesn't have a permit for the gun he used. The storekeeper tells him not to worry, he'll handle it with the cops. Travis flings his gun on the counter as he dashes out. The owner picks up a metal pipe and, in a fit of anger, hits the comatose man again and again.

Swift and brutal, the scene takes care of several fine points of character and narrative. It shows us that Travis is capable of more than target practice, that he doesn't hesitate to pump lead into flesh. For Travis, the junkie is the enemy and therefore not human. Racism plays a part here, just as it did in Vietnam. And it's complicated here, just as it was in Vietnam, where white Americans and Americans of colour fought side by side. Travis and the Puerto Rican storekeeper are united against a common enemy – the black junkie, who's both a predator and an outcast, and definitely lower in the social order than either of them. One could make the case that Travis fired in self-defence. The storekeeper, however, is not defending himself when he beats the unconscious man with a lead pipe. He's taking revenge, not only on this junkie, but also on all the junkies who've tired to rob him in the past. ('Third time this year,' he says as he beats the crumpled body.) Thus the scene demonstrates that racism is not simply a matter of white against black, and that it's not only Travis who flips out when he feels threatened.

The throwaway dialogue about the gun permit and the police also has a narrative purpose. It sets up the idea that there are some crimes the cops are happy to ignore. They'll take the storekeeper's word that he shot the junkie in self-defence. The scene thus supports the logic of the twist at the end, when Travis, rather than being charged with murder, becomes a tabloid hero.

At home, watching *American Bandstand*, Travis leans back in his chair, aiming his gun at a sweetly smiling black kid whose face fills the TV screen. As the TV image widens to show an entire dance floor filled with teenage couples, Travis relaxes his aim, bracing his elbow on the chair arm and holding the gun straight up, so that it brushes the side of his head. Although we see occasional flashes of anger in his eyes, he looks bereft; it's painful for him to watch the easy camaraderie and sexuality of

Lonely boy Travis watching *American Bandstand*

the dancers. This is not Travis the cold gunman of the previous scene, but Travis the lonely guy, who's driven to kill for lack of love. It's one of De Niro's most stunning moments and it's crucial in terms of creating empathy for Travis in the audience

It's late afternoon, maybe the same day, maybe a day later: there's no way to know and it doesn't matter. What matters is that the pressure keeps building within Travis, who's now in his parked cab, watching a Palantine rally on a crowded street in the mid-town garment centre. Palantine is mixing Whitman and the New Testament in a hackneyed speech about the suffering people. ('We the people suffered in Vietnam....') As the camera moves in slow motion among the crowds, the sound becomes muffled as if to suggest Travis's dislocation. We also hear him, in voice-over, composing a letter to his parents. He tells them a fantasy version of his real life, in which Betsy is his girlfriend and he's engaged in top secret government work. The voice-over continues as Travis, now at home, puts the finishing touches on the letter. The television is tuned to a soap opera about a woman who's involved with two men. Travis's foot nudges the TV set until it falls to the floor and explodes. Cradling his head in his hands, he mutters, 'Damn, damn, damn.' There's more troubling him than the broken television.

Travis's paranoia infects the narrative, imbuing seemingly insignificant objects, words and gestures with multiple meanings. Travis writes the letter to his parents on a comic greeting card with the message 'To a couple of good scouts' printed below a cartoon of a middle-aged husband and wife stuffed into boy and girl scout uniforms. But 'scout' is also a word that evokes the nineteenth-century Wild West. As in a western, Travis is scouting for trouble – for violators of law and order – when he patrols New York in his taxi. In the West, there were Indian scouts, pioneer scouts and freelance scouts like Ethan in *The Searchers*, who refuses to obey any law except his own. Triggered by these paranoid associations, the scene shifts from Travis's apartment to the downtown street where twice before Travis encountered Iris, the preteen prostitute. When she appears, he is, as if by magic, at her side. (The magic is in the editing: Scorsese omits the connecting shot of Travis getting out of his cab, as if Travis blacked out in the transition from voyeurism to action.) Iris sends him over to her pimp, Sport, to make the business arrangements.

In her five-inch, orange platform shoes, white hot pants, midriff-baring halter and huge floppy hat, and with her hair tightly waved in the

30s style made popular by *Bonnie and Clyde*, Foster looks spectacular, albeit much too healthy and carefree to have experienced even one day on the stroll, let alone a couple of months. She's a kid playing dress-up, trying to act older than her age. She doesn't seem an obvious choice for an obsessional object. You would have to be Hinckley to know why he wanted her attention so much that he tried to assassinate a president to get it (that is, if there's any truth to his insanity defence).

'These characters are running around and can be triggered by anything, most often by advertisements or innocuous images,' said Schrader, when asked whether his feelings about *Taxi Driver* changed after the Hinckley affair. 'A few years ago they did a study about incitement to rape, and one of the things that cropped up most often was the old Coppertone suntan oil ad – it had a little puppy tugging at a girl's swimsuit. It had just the right mixture for these rapists of adolescent sexuality, female nudity, rear entry, animals, violence.'[28]

Schrader is mistaken in his memory of the illustration, which appeared on thousands of highway billboards and was one of the most celebrated pieces of 50s advertising. The girl wasn't a teenager; she was a three-year-old toddler, whose little ass, dazzlingly white in contrast to her Coppertoned limbs and upper torso, is revealed when the puppy pulls down the back of her swimsuit bottom (the only piece of clothing that she's wearing) with his teeth. Thus the rapists to whom Schrader refers weren't turned on by the suggestion of adolescent sex, but that of paedophilia. In the 50s, the Coppertone baby ad was considered cute. Today, with child abuse in the forefront of American consciousness, no advertising agency would dare to produce it.

What's curious about Schrader's statement is that he seems never to have encountered the popular misidentification of Jodie Foster as the model for the Coppertone baby. The spokesperson for Scherring Plough Inc., the advertising agency that produced the ad, was happy to have this opportunity to set the record straight. Foster wasn't born until a decade after the ad was produced. Joyce Ballantyne, the illustrator, used her own daughter, Cherri Brand, as the model. But Foster's first professional job as an actress was indeed in a TV commercial for Coppertone and she was about three years old at the time. Hence the confusion.

Schrader and Scorsese both say that they knew nothing about Foster's history with Coppertone. Scorsese had already worked with Foster in *Alice Doesn't Live Here Anymore*. He thought she was a terrific young actress and had the unflappable quality he wanted for Iris. Still, Foster and Coppertone, and the Coppertone ad as part of a psychological test for psychopaths such as Hinckley, are connected in a way that seems like an extension of the kind of paranoid syndrome which shapes the narrative of the film.

Travis approaches Sport, who gives him the once-over and accuses him of being a cop. There is an immediate animosity between them. In terms of their individual styles of machismo, they are as opposite as Scorsese and Schrader. Sport is all nervous energy – he never stops talking and moving – even if he's only shifting his weight from one foot to the other. Travis's eyes are stone cold and his body is so tight with anger that he looks like metal wind-up toy. Sport knows that something about Travis is not right, but he can't pin it down. He starts needling him about being a cowboy after he notices his western boots. But, if Travis is a cowboy, then Sport, with his straight, black, shoulder-length hair, his bandana and beads, and his hippie vest that leaves his sinewy arms bare, is an Indian. Scorsese plays up the parallel between the triangle of Travis, Sport and Iris, and that of Ethan, Scar and Debbie in *The Searchers*. Travis, the

cowboy, comes to rescue Iris, the maiden, whom Sport, the Indian, has defiled. Travis follows Iris up the stairs of a tenement building and into a room that's decorated like a hippie pad with beaded curtains, coloured paper lampshades and dozens of candles. Iris wants to get down to business. She starts pulling off her shirt and asking Travis how he wants to make it. Travis is horrified, but he doesn't back off from his rescue mission. Iris thinks, at first, that he's just a timid john who needs encouragement, but eventually she realises that he's not interested in sex and that he really wants to help her. She thanks him for his concern and explains that if she leaves she has nowhere else to go. Travis asks her to meet him the next day. When Iris suggests a one o'clock breakfast, Travis hesitates, remembering something else he has to do – something no doubt involving Palantine. But then he agrees. Travis needs to be saved as much as Iris does, and for a moment it seems possible for him to forge with her the friendship that he desperately needs. Travis is more spontaneous and lighter in spirit in this scene than we've ever seen him. Because Iris is as powerless as he is, he feels none of the anger that he felt towards Betsy. As he leaves her room, we hear a few bars of the soaring saxophone theme. Then, at the far end of

Travis the cowboy and Sport the Indian

the dark hallway, Travis sees an emissary from hell. It's merely Iris's decrepit timekeeper looking for his tip, but the contact is enough to destroy Travis's romantic fantasy. The music turns dark: the corridor looks, even more than it did when Travis followed Iris inside, like the setting of a horror movie. This is the tenement where the massacre will take place, and Scorsese is giving us a preview of things to come.

But it's bright sunlight when Travis meets Iris in a grimy twenty-four-hour coffee shop on the corner of East 14th Street, where, for a decade, hookers, pimps, junkies and retirees from the East Village crossed paths with the kids who went to rock concerts a few doors away at the Palladium. What Scorsese and Schrader wanted to show through these downtown locations is the demise of the 60s counterculture, but what we see on screen is almost indistinguishable from Times Square sleaze. Like the earlier coffee shop scene with Betsy, this one is staged very simply with two-shots, reverse angles and medium close-ups. Iris is munching toast with jam, topped off with a layer of sugar. Whenever Travis probes too hard, she becomes intent on her food, and, behind her dollar shades, her eyes turn stony. She and Travis have a surprisingly easy rapport – he lectures her as if she were his kid sister. The scene is like a reprieve – for both Travis and the audience. It sets up the false hope that the project of saving Iris will replace the plan to assassinate Palantine. But unlike Debbie (Natalie Wood) in *The Searchers*, Iris wasn't kidnapped. She ran away from home. And home is no longer the place of refuge it was in John Ford's myth of America – not even in Travis's fantasy. So when Iris says she'd rather go to a commune in Vermont, he offers her the bus fare. He's fixated on getting her away from Sport; what happens to her after that seems not to interest him very much. 'Someone has to do something about him. He's the worst sucking scum. You can't allow him to do to other girls what he did to you.' An idea is roiling in Travis's brain, but he hasn't quite made the connections. Sport is the scum that needs to be washed from the street. Iris can't do anything. The cops will not do anything. So who does that leave?

Travis is parked outside the building where Iris takes her customers. He's looking up at her window and popping pills. Inside Iris's apartment, she's slow dancing with Sport who is trying to placate her –

Sport slow dancing with Iris

telling her how much he loves and needs her. The scene was added at Scorsese's insistence and despite Schrader's reservations about departing from Travis's point of view at such a crucial point in the narrative. Scorsese tries to suggest that the scene may be Travis's fantasy by cutting from Travis looking up at Iris's window to Iris and Sport inside, and also by having them dance to the romantic saxophone theme which we last heard when Travis left Iris's apartment. Sport puts a record on the turntable and out pours Bernard Herrmann. The strategy is not completely convincing, although Travis's position as the third party in what's essentially an oedipal triangle (he's the child who's been left out in the cold, spying at the door) replicates the position of the pyscho passenger secretly spying on his wife, as well as Travis's own position in relation to the couples in the porn movies. Unlike the passenger who wanted to blow away both his wife and her lover, Travis fantasises about killing Sport in order to save Iris.

Scorsese claims the scene was needed to show that Iris was not being held against her will, that she got something she needed from the relationship with Sport. He also claims that Sport half-believes what he tells Iris and therefore that the scene proves he's a more complicated character than we might have supposed.

Something else, however, is going on here. On a practical level, Scorsese must have felt obligated to beef up Keitel's role, which otherwise would have consisted of only his two scenes with De Niro. (Keitel, after all, was the star of *Mean Streets*.) But Scorsese was also fascinated by the sado-masochist dynamic between an under-aged girl and an adult bad guy. The fantasy of sexual coercion played out here takes an even more perverse form in the scene in the school basement in *Cape Fear* (1991), where De Niro mesmerises Juliette Lewis and gets her to suck his finger. Thelma Schoonmaker, who has edited all of Scorsese's films from *Raging Bull* (1980) on, says that that was the scene in the script which sold Scorsese on doing *Cape Fear*. Just as Travis identifies with Iris's masochistic position, Scorsese identifies with that of the Juliette Lewis character. (*Cape Fear* is a much more interesting film when it's read through the young girl's subjectivity – as a narrative of female sexuality and coming to power.) But Travis also desires to be Sport – to have his power over women. The homoeroticism embedded in that desire is what Travis must destroy in order to convince himself of his masculinity. And the only way for Travis to do this is to kill Sport.

Travis is not ready, however, to give up his original plan. He's like someone who holds on to a doomed love affair, even after he's become involved in one that seems more promising. As if the film itself were urging Travis to get back on track, the sound of gunfire cuts through the close-up of Iris and Sport dancing, and we're again with Travis in the midst of preparing for war. The sequence begins with target practice and then shifts to Travis's apartment, where he is dressing for what he expects will be his last day on earth. The new element in the montage is fire. Travis heats tins of boot polish and burns dead flowers (relics of his failed courtship of Betsy). The music is more dissonant and chaotic than ever before, filled with clashing cymbals and ominous, rippling scales on the harp and vibraphone. This is blatant horror-film music, and we'll hear it again in the aftermath of the massacre. Having strapped on his weapons, Travis places cash and a note in an envelope addressed to Iris. In his crisp, white shirt, he looks for a moment like a guy getting ready for a date; to underline the effect, a few bars of the romantic saxophone theme cuts into the horror music . But there is no respite for Travis. 'Now I see it clearly. My whole life has pointed in one direction. There has never been any choice for me,' he says in voice-over, as the scene shifts to a Palantine rally at Columbus Circle.

Travis pushes through the crowd, ready to draw

Travis is lurking at the edge of the rally crowd, popping pills. He has shaved his head, Mohawk style, leaving only a strip of hair running from forehead to the nape of the neck. (De Niro and Scorsese learned from one of the stunt men on the film that, in Vietnam, guys in Special Forces gave themselves mohicans on the eve of a dangerous mission. The mohican was a sign that they were in killer mode and should be left alone.) The effect is startling – as if Travis had finally broken with any semblance of sanity and was now totally in the grip of his psychosis. Palantine has launched into his 'We the people' spiel and Travis applauds every turn of phrase, his manic smile contorting his face. Since Travis's dress and demeanour proclaim his alienation from the human race, it's understandable that Palantine's cheery invocation of the power of the people would enrage him. As Palantine leaves the speakers' platform, Travis pushes through the crowd, reaching inside his King Kong company jacket for his gun. He's spotted by the Secret Service men, who give chase.

Back in his apartment, Travis is shirtless, pacing like a frustrated animal in a zoo cage, tossing down pills with beer, shaking his head in a frenzy. The chaotic music starts again and bridges a change of location to the front steps of a building where Sport is transacting business. We can read the shot of Sport as Travis's projection (he knows where Sport is and what he's doing); it's the sign that, having failed to kill Palantine, Travis is focused on a new target.

And, sure enough, Travis is hurtling downtown in what is now unequivocally the cab from hell. The street, the cab and Travis's face seen through the windshield are tinted phosphorescent green. In profile, Travis's shaved head looks like a diminutive version of Max Schrenk's in *Nosferatu*. This greenish shot is a transition between the gleaming, saturated primary colours of the film thus far and the dirty, almost monochromatic palette of the massacre sequence. After *Taxi Driver* was completed, it was submitted to the MPAA ratings board, which refused to give it an 'R' unless Scorsese trimmed some of the blood. He came up with an alternative – making the blood less red – and the quixotic MPAA accepted this. Schrader and cinematographer Michael Chapman objected vehemently. They wanted fresh crimson. Scorsese, on the other hand, now says that if he had had a bigger budget he would have processed the rest of the film the way he did the massacre scene.

Optically printed on a sandwich of black-and-white and colour stocks (the balance of which was altered shot to shot), the sequence has a grainy, degraded tabloid look. The difference in colour, density and grain is barely discernible on the home video, laserdisc and DVD versions, but on the movie screen, even in faded prints, the effect is stunning. Contemporary audiences are eager to laugh at *Taxi Driver*'s mordant humour (proving that their capacity for denial is as great as that of the characters in the film who think of Travis as 'a funny guy'); however, from the moment Travis steps from his cab to confront Sport for the last time to the backward tracking shots at the end of the massacre, they sit silently, as if in a collective trance.

It's suddenly apparent that the entire film has existed for the purpose of this sudden change of register. Scorsese employs the same strategy at the climax of *Kundun* (1997) and of *Goodfellas*. Like Travis's homicidal rage, the Dalai Lama's spiritual transcendence and Henry Hill's cocaine-induced psychosis are reflected in set pieces that have the intensity and hallucinatory quality of dreams. But Travis, who's an insomniac, doesn't dream. He goes to porn movies instead. As he bounds from his cab to confront Sport, he must feel as if he's walking into one of those movies. ('I felt like I was walking into a movie,' said John Hinckley at his trial, trying to explain his state of mind when he attempted to assassinate Ronald Reagan, the actor-president.) The music drops away, the colour fades and Travis, moving fast, is in Sport's face, clapping him on the shoulder, jawing with him, then stepping back, pulling out a gun, sticking it into Sport's gut, and pulling the trigger. 'Suck on this,' mutters Travis, as he shoots. It's a familiar enough tough guy expression, but the double entendre clinches the connection between the bloodletting, the porn movie running in Travis's brain and the castration anxiety and homophobia erupting from his tortured unconscious. The sequence is framed in wide-angle and the camera doesn't budge, which makes it all the more hallucinatory. Because there's no close-up of the gun as it's fired, we're not sure of what we've seen. There's a delay between perception and cognition. Things have gone out of whack.

After Sport falls, Travis sits on the next-door stoop to collect himself. Then he enters the tenement where Iris has her room. Coming toward him is Iris's timekeeper. Travis shoots and the bullet blows three fingers off the timekeeper's hand. This time, Scorsese goes in for the close-up. The hand is a now a red stump and the blood is splattered on the walls and on Travis's face. As the sound of the bullet echoes though the hall, Travis is shot in the neck by Sport who is at the far end of the lobby

'I'll kill you, I'll kill you'

Travis is winged

corridor just inside the doorway. Travis whirls and fires on Sport, then staggers down the hall, puts several more bullets in Sport, drops the empty .44 Magnum on the floor, comes back and shoots the timekeeper again. But the timekeeper refuses to die and keeps coming after Travis, who is mounting the stairs towards Iris. The timekeeper is yelling 'I'll kill you, I'll kill you', over and over again. Another man (we saw him earlier collecting money from Sport) creeps up behind Travis and wings him. Travis falls to the ground holding his bloody neck; with his other hand, he flips the gun from his arm brace and fires a full round into the man who falls backwards through the doorway of Iris's room and lands dead at her feet. Iris is screaming; the timekeeper is still yelling 'I'll kill you' as he hurls himself on Travis, hanging onto his back. Travis crawls into Iris's room trying to throw the timekeeper off. They wrestle clumsily on the floor until Travis pulls his Bowie knife (named for James Bowie, one of the heroes of the Alamo) from his boot and stabs the timekeeper through the hand. Then, as Iris screams 'don't shoot him', he blows the timekeeper's head apart. We hear the sound of dripping blood, as Travis pulls himself to his feet, places the gun against his own neck and fires. Alas, the gun is empty. He tries again with another gun, but that one is empty, too. Travis slowly eases himself down on the end of the couch; Iris crouches motionless on the other end. Travis's head falls backward. It is silent in the room for several seconds. Then, the music starts again. It's the same annunciatory brass and percussion riff that we heard at the opening of the title sequence of the film, and it suggests that the film has come full circle, that we should have known from the very first shot that it would come to this. Two cops appear in the doorway, their guns pointed at Travis. Travis raises his head, places his bloody finger against his head and mimes shooting himself three times. The camera is tight on Travis's blood-splattered face; blood is dripping in gobs from between his fingers; and, deep in his throat, he's making the sound of a gunshot as he mimes pulling the trigger. The cops, however, do not take the hint. They stand frozen, holding their fire as Travis's head falls back on the couch.

Suddenly, we're looking down on the carnage from a great height. If the grand-guignol close-up of Travis's face as he mimes shooting himself is the culmination of all the mock shootings we've seen throughout the film, then this overhead tracking shot is the pay-off for all the overhead shots which were signs of Travis's momentary disassociation. Now, it's as if he has left his body and this earth for good. If you've intuited Scorsese's association of the overhead shots with looking down at the objects on the altar during the mass, then this high-angle, backward tracking shot could be the equivalent of the terrifying line in the Apostle's creed, 'He will come again in glory to judge the living and the dead.' Certainly, to look down is a sign of judgment, though who or what is judging is up for grabs.

The overhead shot continues until it's just outside Iris's doorway, and then it dissolves into a series of more modest backward tracks that take in the blood-splattered walls and the discarded guns, as if they marked the stations of the cross. Pausing over Sport's bloody corpse sprawled in the doorway, the camera finally makes it way onto the street, where crowds have gathered and cop cars race, in slow motion, towards the scene.

From the moment Travis leaves his cab to the moment the camera re-emerges from the house, slightly less than seven minutes have passed. You would never know that, however, without looking at your watch. The sequence seems to exist outside of time. Without being in the least overblown, it has a religious majesty that's unique in American movies. Gory and elegant, violent and voluptuous, kinetic and visceral, realistic and hallucinatory, it's pervaded by a sense of inevitability and, beyond that, by a sense of *déjà vu*. We have been so primed for this moment that it seems almost as if it has all happened before. In a way, it has. We've been on the stoop with Sport, we've been inside that building, we've gone up and down the stairs, we've hung out in Iris's room. Similarly, we've watched Travis rehearse every move he makes during the massacre. What's new is the blood, but we saw that coming.

'My whole life has pointed in one direction,' says Travis, as he goes out to shoot Palantine. But Palantine is inaccessible, so instead he kills three scuzzballs in a whorehouse. It doesn't matter who he kills. What matters is the eruption of violence, the return of the repressed, the endless cycle. That is why the film cannot let Travis die. *Taxi Driver* is not merely a portrait of Travis Bickle. It's also about a syndrome of violence that recurs throughout history and whose mantra is 'I'll kill you, I'll kill you'. The violence erupts out of a terrible anxiety about masculinity and about the loss of power and not being on top. And because anxiety can be eradicated only by death, the violence tends towards the apocalyptic.

The apocalpyse, however, does not happen for Travis, as it has not happened for so many who've prayed for it or who've tried to bring it on with bloodshed. The nightmare America deserves, Travis is resurrected as a tabloid hero, the saviour of a twelve-year-old girl who had been kidnapped into white slavery. The camera pans across a set of newspaper clippings tacked to the wall, as we hear Iris's father reading a letter thanking Travis for their daughter's safe return.

Travis is standing with a bunch of other drivers outside a fashionable hotel waiting for fares. A woman gets into Travis's cab. It's Betsy. Travis's expression shifts between hostility and triumph, as Betsy quizzes him about the shoot-out and his new hero status. Travis has put Betsy behind him, and that's literally how we see her in the scene, as a disembodied reflection in his rear-view mirror (a bit player in his New York movie) and, then, standing alone on the street as Travis's cab pulls away. Travis may have gotten over Betsy, he may have been lauded as a hero, his anger may have been spent for the moment, but there are signs that he's as much of a time bomb as ever. The last we see of Travis is a close-up of his darting paranoid eyes in the rear-view mirror. As the end credits crawl up the screen, we continue to see the night lights of New York from Travis's perspective, through the front windshield. Just before the image fades, there's a change of direction and a yellow cab comes towards us and disappears out the lower left corner of the frame. It's a wider version of the film's opening shot. As an extra touch of horror, or perhaps an ironic reminder that what we've seen is only a movie, the last three chords of the score are a quote from the end of *Psycho*.[29]

. . . .

Taxi Driver opened on 8 February 1976 at the Coronet theatre where it broke the first- and second-day box-office records. It went on to become the twelfth-highest-grossing film of the year in the United States. The reviews from the influential critics were more favourable than not. Pauline Kael in the *New Yorker* and Frank Rich, then a film critic for the *New York Post*, filed raves. Vincent Canby in the *New York Times* and Andrew Sarris in the *Village Voice* were also enthusiastic, although both expressed some qualms about the violence. Writing collaboratively in *Film Comment*, however, Manny Farber and Patricia Patterson launched a scathing attack,[30] faulting the film for its inconsistent portrayal of a psychopath and De Niro for relying on his movie-star glamour. They were particularly outraged by the lack of truth in the depiction of cab driving as labour and by Scorsese's glib French New Wave references. Later, and in a more academic context, Robin Wood attacked the film's liberalism in reducing the failure of the 60s and its aftermath to one man's personal crisis.[31]

If the film was attacked most vehemently from the left, it found little support in mainstream Hollywood. Although it received four Oscar nominations (for best picture, best actor, best supporting actress and best score), it won nothing. *Rocky*, a more soothing vision of masculine triumph, was named best picture and its director, John G. Avildsen, also took home an Oscar. Scorsese was not even nominated. The Cannes Film Festival, however, which periodically has looked favourably on the depiction of American male angst, awarded it the 1976 Palme d'Or, thus boosting its world-wide box office and putting Scorsese on the international cinema map. (The other American Palme d'Or winners are *Marty*, (1954), *Friendly Persuasion* (1956), and, more significantly in the post-*Taxi Driver* period, *Apocalypse Now* (1979), *sex, lies and videotape* (1989), *Wild at Heart* (1990), and *Pulp Fiction* (1994).)

Although the Hinckley incident exposed the power of the film on the collective cultural consciousness (and hugely boosted video rentals), it was not the first time Travis's madness had bled to real life. In Scorsese's files is a clipping from the New York newspaper the *Daily News*, dated 14 May 1976, about a man in Norfolk, Virginia, who walked into a bar and fatally shot four people before killing himself. The headline of the piece is 'Death Wish in Va.', but what the man said before firing – that he had come to clean out pimps, prostitutes and dope pushers – is too close to Travis's words for comfort. Scorsese and Schrader at various times have remarked that they were disturbed by the way some audiences responded to the violence; after Hinckley's assassination attempt, Scorsese briefly thought about giving up film-making.[32] Instead he made *The King of Comedy* (1982).

The first US independent film to blatantly display the influence of *Taxi Driver*'s kinetic and visceral punch, as well as its depiction of masculinity through blood-letting was Quentin Tarantino's *Reservoir Dogs* (1992), after which the floodgates opened, and not only in America. Mathieu Kassovitz's *La Haine* (1995) is an example of Bickle worship at its most disturbing. *Taxi Driver* even infected Hollywood studio films; David Peoples, who wrote the screenplay for

Unforgiven (1992), claimed that Travis was an influence on Clint Eastwood's exhausted gunslinger.

An enigma and a piece of common knowledge, Travis Bickle is lodged in the collective cultural consciousness to a degree that makes an aesthetic evaluation of *Taxi Driver* almost irrelevant. In its hall of mirrors, perhaps the strangest reflection involves the heroising and fetishisation of Travis both within the film and without. The answer to critics who find the open ending dubious on both moral and logical grounds is what has happened in the near twenty-five years since the film's release.

NOTES

· ·

1 From my interviews with Paul Schrader between 1995 and 1998. Many of these details are also in Richard Thompson's interview with Schrader in *Film Comment*, March–April 1976, and on the second track of the Voyager laserdisc of *Taxi Driver*, where Schrader and Scorsese conduct a running commentary on the film.

2 Arthur H. Bremer, *An Assassin's Diary* (New York: Harper's Magazine Press, 1974). Excerpts from the diary were published in *Harper's* magazine in January 1973. Schrader says that when he finally read *An Assassin's Diary*, he was surprised at the number of similarities between Bremer's text and the *Taxi Driver* screenplay. In the *Film Comment* interview, he remarks that he had considered lifting a few lines, but he refrained, for fear that Bremer, who was sitting in jail with nothing but time on his hands, would sue.

3 In most interviews, Schrader says that the first full draft of the script was written in ten days, but the full draft was preceded by a seventy-five page outline which took about five days to write. In any event, the initial script was written in a fairly short period of time, probably no more than fifteen days.

4 Paul Schrader, *Taxi Driver* (London: Faber & Faber, 1990), p. 86.

5 Martin Scorsese interviewed by Richard Goldstein and Mark Jacobson, *Village Voice*, 5 April 1976.

6 *Schrader on Schrader*, ed. Kevin Jackson (London: Faber & Faber, 1990), p. 115. Also Julia Phillips, *You'll Never Eat Lunch in This Town Again* (New York: Random House, 1991).

7 Stephen Rebello, *Alfred Hitchcock and the Making of Psycho* (New York: Harper Perennial, 1991).

8 David Wojnarowicz, *Fever: The Art of David Wojnarowicz*, ed. Amy Scholder (New York: New Museum Books, 1999).

9 'Notes on Noir' was originally published in 1971 as a catalogue essay for the Los Angeles Film Festival. It was reprinted in *Film Comment*, Spring 1972; and in *Schrader on Schrader*.

10 Susan Faludi's *Stiffed* (New York: Willam Morrow, 1999), although confused as a feminist analysis, brings a historical perspective to the current crisis surrounding masculinity.

11 The .44 Magnum speech in Don Siegel's *Dirty Harry* (1971) is generally attributed to Milius, who wrote an uncredited draft of the script. (See Carlos Clarens. *Crime Movies* (New York: Norton, 1980).) In the early 70s, Milius, Schrader and Scorsese were part of a loose knit group of directors who were trying to take advantage of the turmoil in the studio system to become auteurs in Hollywood. Milius and Schrader were both obsessed with guns.

12 My interview with Scorsese in 1993.

13 My interview with Schrader in 1995.

14 Ibid.

15 James Quant (ed.), *Robert Bresson* (Toronto: Cinemathèque Ontario,1998).

16 Hal Lindsey, *The Late Great Planet Earth* (Grand Rapids: Zondervan Publishing, 1970).

17 My interview with Scorsese in 1993.

18 Ibid.

19 *Taxi Driver*, p. xvi.

20 *Schrader on Schrader*, p.155.

21 Graham Bruce, *Bernard Herrmann: Film Music and Narration* (Ann Arbor: UMI Research Press, 1985).

22 *Taxi Driver*, The Criterion Collection Video Laser Disk, produced in 1990 by the Voyager Company, Santa Monica, California.

23 Richard Slotkin, *Gunfighter Nation*, *The Myth of the Frontier in Twentieth-Century America* (New York: Atheneum, 1992, republished by University of Oklahoma Press, 1998).

24 Scorsese later made the short documentary *American Boy* about Steven Prince, a middle-class drop-out drug dealer, who had figured in his thinking about Travis Bickle.

25 In Christopher Sharrett (ed.), *Crisis Cinema*, *The Apocalyptic Idea in Postmodern American Film* (Washington DC: Maisoneuve Press, 1993).

26 Laura Mulvey, *Fetishism and Curiosity* (Bloomington: BFI/Indiana University Press, 1996).

27 Robert Warshow, 'The Westerner', *Partisan Review*, March 1954.

28 *Schrader on Schrader*, p. 120.

29 The film's open ending did not extended to
Bernhard Herrmann, who died in his sleep on 24
December 1975, just hours after he finished the
orchestral recording of the score.

30 Patricia Patterson and Manny Farber, 'The
Power and the Gory', *Film Comment*, May–June
1976.

31 Robin Wood, *Hollywood from Vietnam to
Reagan* (New York: Columbia University Press,
1986).

32 J. Hoberman, 'King of Outsiders', *Village
Voice*, 15 February 1983.

CREDITS

· ·

Taxi Driver

USA
1976

Production Companies
Columbia Pictures presents
an Italo-Judeo production
A Bill/Phillips production
A Martin Scorsese film
Producers
Michael Phillips
Julia Phillips
Associate Producer
Phillip M. Goldfarb
Production Office
Co-ordinator
Noni Rock
Production Services
Devon/Persky-Bright
Assistant to the
Producers
Keith Addis
Production Assistants
Eugene Iemola, Gary
Springer, Chris Soldo
Secretaries to the
Producers
Renate Rupp, Pat Dodds
Director
Martin Scorsese
Assistant Director
Peter R. Scoppa
2nd Assistant Directors
Ralph Singleton,
William Eustace
DGA Trainee
Robert Cohen
Assistant to the Director
Amy Jones
Script Supervisor
Kay Chapin
Casting
Juliet Taylor
Atmosphere Casting
Sylvia Faye
Screenplay
Paul Schrader
Director of Photography
Michael Chapman

2nd Unit Camera
Michael Zingale
Camera Operator
Fred Schuler
Assistant Camera
Alec Hirshfeld, Bill Johnson,
Ron Zarilla
Key Grip
Robert Ward
Grip
Edward Quinn
Gaffer
Richard Quinlan
Best Boy
Billy Ward
Special Photography
Steve Shapiro
Still Photography
Josh Weiner
Special Effects
Tony Parmelee
Supervising Editor
Marcia Lucas
Editors
Tom Rolf, Melvin Shapiro
Assistant Editors
George Trirogoff,
William Weber
Visual Consultant
David Nichols
Art Director
Charles Rosen
Set Decorator
Herbert Mulligan
Scenic Artist
Cosmo Sorice
Property Master
Les Bloom
Assistant Property
Master
Dave Goodnoff
Costume Designer
Ruth Morley
Wardrobe
Al Craine
Special Make-up
Dick Smith

Make-up
Irving Buchman
Hairdresser
Mona Orr
Title Design
Dan Perri
Optical Effects
M.G.M.
Music
Bernard Herrmann
Music Arrangers/
Conductors
Dave Blume,
Bernard Herrmann
Solo Sax
Ronnie Lang
Music Editor
Shinichi Yamazaki
Soundtrack
'Late for the Sky' by Jackson
Browne; 'Hold Me Close' by
Keith Addis (lyrics),
Bernard Herrmann (music),
sung by George (Oobie)
McKern
Recordist
Roger Pietschman
Boom Man
Robert Rogow
Mixer
Les Lazarowitz
Re-recording Supervisor
Tex Rudloff
Re-recording Mixers
Dick Alexander, Vern Poore
Supervising Sound
Effects Editor
Frank E. Warner
Sound Effects Editors
Sam Gemette, Jim Fritch,
David Horton, Gordon
Davidson
Creative Consultant
Sandra Weintraub
Transportation
Co-ordinator
Ray Hartwick

Publicist
Howard Newman
Special Publicity
Marion Billings
With Thanks to
Julia Cameron, Dick Clark
Productions, Loretta
Cubberley, Richard
Goodwin, Kris
Kristofferson, Charlie
McCarthy, Jerry Orange,
Hank Phillippi, Jack Hayes,
Linda Kopcyk

'Our gratitude and respect to
Bernard Herrmann, June 29
1911–December 24 1975'

Robert De Niro
Travis Bickle
Cybill Shepherd
Betsy
Jodie Foster
Iris
Peter Boyle
Wizard
Leonard Harris
Charles Palantine
Harvey Keitel
Sport
Martin Scorsese
passenger watching
silhouette
Steven Prince
Andy, gun salesman

Diahnne Abbot
concession girl
Frank Adu
angry black man
Vic Argo
Melio
Gino Ardito
policeman at rally
Garth Avery
Iris's friend
Albert Brooks
Tom
Harry Cohn
cabbie in Bellmore
Copper Cunningham
hooker in cab
Brenda Dickson
soap opera woman
Harry Fischler
dispatcher
Nat Grant
stick-up man
Richard Higgs
tall Secret Service man
Beau Kayser
soap opera man
Vic Magnotta
Secret Service photographer
Robert Maroff
mafioso
Norman Matlock
Charlie T.
Bill Minkin
Tom's assistant
Murray Mosten
Iris's time keeper

Harry Northup
doughboy
Gene Palma
street drummer
Carey Poe
campaign worker
Peter Savage
the John
Robert Shields
Palantine aide
Ralph Singleton
TV interviewer
Joe Spinell
personnel officer
Maria Turner
angry hooker on street
Robin Utt
campaign worker

10,277 feet
114 minutes

Colour by
Metrocolor

Credits compiled by Markku
Salmi, BFI Filmographic
Unit.

The print of *Taxi Driver* in
the National Film and
Television Archive was
acquired specially for the 360
Classic Feature Films project
from Columbia Pictures,
California.

ALSO PUBLISHED

If you would like further information about future BFI Film Classics or about other books on film, media and popular culture from BFI Publishing, please write to:

BFI Film Classics
BFI Publishing
21 Stephen Street
London W1P 2LN

BFI Film Classics '...could scarcely be improved upon ... informative, intelligent, jargon-free companions.'
The Observer

Each book in the BFI Publishing Film Classics series honours a great film from the history of world cinema. With new titles published each year, the series is rapidly building into a collection representing some of the best writing on film. If you would like to receive further information about future Film Classics or about other books on film, media and popular culture from BFI Publishing, please fill in your name and address and return this card to the BFI.* (No stamp required if posted in the UK, Channel Islands, or Isle of Man.)

NAME

ADDRESS

POSTCODE

WHICH *BFI FILM CLASSIC* DID YOU BUY?

* In North America, please return your card to: Indiana University Press, Attn: LPB, 601 N. Morton Street, Bloomington, IN 47401-3797